GW01454855

Month / Year

_____

This workbook+planner belongs to:

_____

If lost, contact:

_____

Copyright © 2021 by Kathy Oneto.

All rights reserved. No part of this publication may be reproduced, distributed or transmitted in any form or by any means, including photocopying, recording, or other electronic or mechanical methods, without the prior written permission of the publisher, except in the case of brief quotations embodied in critical reviews and certain other non-commercial uses permitted by copyright law. For permission requests, write to the author, at: kathyoneto@sustainableambition.com.

Kathy Oneto

Sustainable Ambition Press

https://sustainableambition.com

Sustainable Ambition / Kathy Oneto —1st ed.

Paperback ISBN 979-8-9853093-0-0

Sustainable Ambition

12-Month Workbook+Planner:
Your Life+Work Resilience Rx

A workbook+planner to help you lead a
fulfilling, sustainable, and ambitious life+work

SA SUSTAINABLE
AMBITION™

What is Sustainable Ambition?

Sustainable Ambition offers a strategic approach to life+work integration. It is about crafting a fulfilling career to support your life from decade to decade. The end goal—experience more fulfillment in your professional and personal life with more ease, while still being ambitious.

In that, you might notice that Sustainable Ambition has two parts. The first is managing a career over time. The second is managing life+work in the current moment. This workbook+planner is meant to help with the second part, managing a more sustainable life+work over twelve to eighteen months.

Now, Sustainable Ambition is aspirational. It asks us to hold two opposing ideas—sustain and stretch—at the same time. How can we sustain ourselves (sustainable), while stretching ourselves (ambition)? That implies it is a practice that calls for perspective, personalization, pacing, and patience. And that admittedly means it isn't easy! It takes learning about ourselves, planning, practicing, and progressing. Again, where this workbook+planner comes in.

Why the Sustainable Ambition Workbook+Planner?

Many of us juggle life+work and seek to find a rhythm that works for us not against us. If you're picking up this workbook+planner, you might be asking yourself, "How do I bring more sustainability to my life+work, because what I'm doing right now just isn't sustainable any more?" In today's modern world that demands too much of us, it's easy to understand how many of us get to this point—it's unsustainable, and we're bordering on burnout. Or, you might be someone who is leading a full life+work and wants to know how to better manage your stretching activities while sustaining yourself.

And that's just it—we want to stretch ourselves and want to have ambitions, yet how can we do so while sustaining ourselves?

We've all heard the call for "work-life balance," but despite the barriers we all know exist, expecting our external world to magically produce balance is a false expectation. It is rare that we experience balance, and certainly not all of the time. It assumes we live in a static environment that allows us to always be in equilibrium. But that isn't today's modern, dynamic world.

So we champion: don't expect work-life balance—build life+work resilience instead.

With this workbook+planner, the intention is to foster the ability to dance in our dynamic world, learning how to both sustain and stretch ourselves.

How? By defining your own Life+Work Resilience Rx (prescription), creating a plan, practicing, and progressing over time.

Not only will it put you on a path towards more sustainability, you just might find that it helps you operate at your best, reach your full potential, and enjoy more life+work fulfillment.

"You can do anything you set your mind to."

BENJAMIN FRANKLIN

Contents

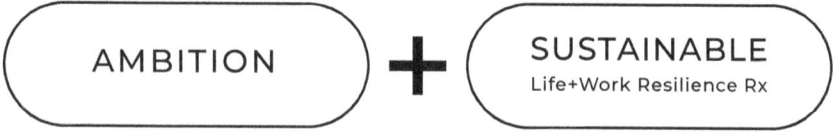

AMBITION **+** SUSTAINABLE
Life+Work Resilience Rx

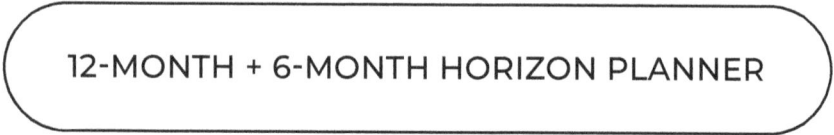

12-MONTH + 6-MONTH HORIZON PLANNER

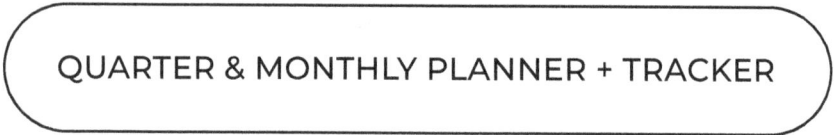

QUARTER & MONTHLY PLANNER + TRACKER

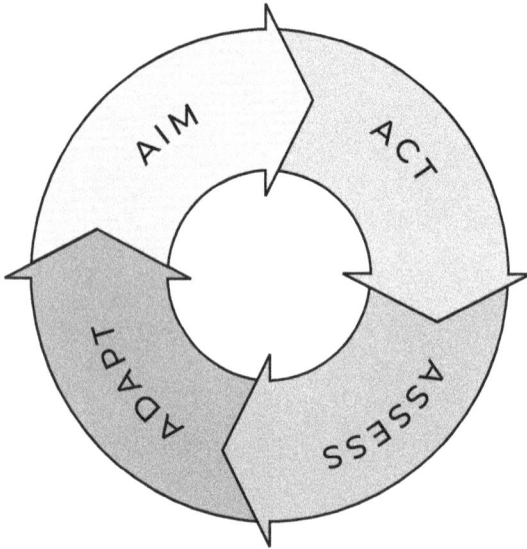

AIM · ACT · ASSESS · ADAPT

WEEKLY & DAILY CHECK-INS

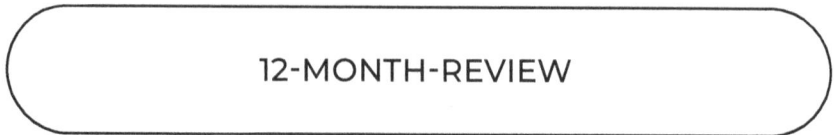

12-MONTH-REVIEW

Are you ready to take back control and plan a more ambitious and sustainable life+work for the 12-months ahead? It's possible, but guess what? It takes knowing yourself better, some planning, practicing, and progressing over time. This workbook and planner will guide and support you to understand what will be stretching for you and what will sustain you.

The workbook+planner guide you to:

SECTION 1:   Set a vision and your intentions—what are your ambitions?

SECTION 2:   Explore what would make your life+work sustainable— what is your personal Life+Work Resilience Rx?

SECTION 3:   Create your 12-month plan and look forward another 6 months—what do you need on your calendar to allow you to stretch and sustain yourself?

SECTIONS 4-7: Aim, Act, Assess, and Adapt on a quarterly and monthly basis—what do you plan, practice, and then progress to operate at your best throughout the year?

SECTION 8:   Check-in weekly and daily—are you staying on track?

SECTION 9:   Conduct a 12-month review—when you pause and reflect, what did you learn about building your own life+work resilience?

Work with the workbook+planner over the course of the 12 months. Start by completing Sections 1, 2, and 3, which are the foundation. Then work through the remaining planner sections over the coming months.

While a sustainable and ambitious life+work is aspirational, the journey may not always be easy along the way. Yet, we believe you can do it and find your way. You can take back control and be in choice to build a more sustainable life+work. We know you got this. Let's go!

"A [person] who does not plan long ahead will find trouble at his door."

CONFUCIUS

Reference Tools

For resources that complement the workbook+planner go to:

www.sustainableambition.com/planner

There you'll find:

- Workbook+Planner Examples
- Planning Guides
- Productivity Tips
- Reference Books
- And more

The workbook+planner can be used by you on your own, or you can create a circle of friends or professional colleagues to plan and learn together. Doing this work as part of a community can support you in setting intentions, holding yourself accountable, providing encouragement, and learning together along the way.

At www.sustainableambition.com/planner, we provide Planning Guides to host your own planning circle or workshop:

- Personal: Hold a Sustainable Ambition Planning Circle
- Professional: Hold a Sustainable Ambition Workshop at Work

Learn more about Sustainable Ambition at: SustainableAmbition.com

Listen to The Sustainable Ambition Podcast on your favorite podcast player.

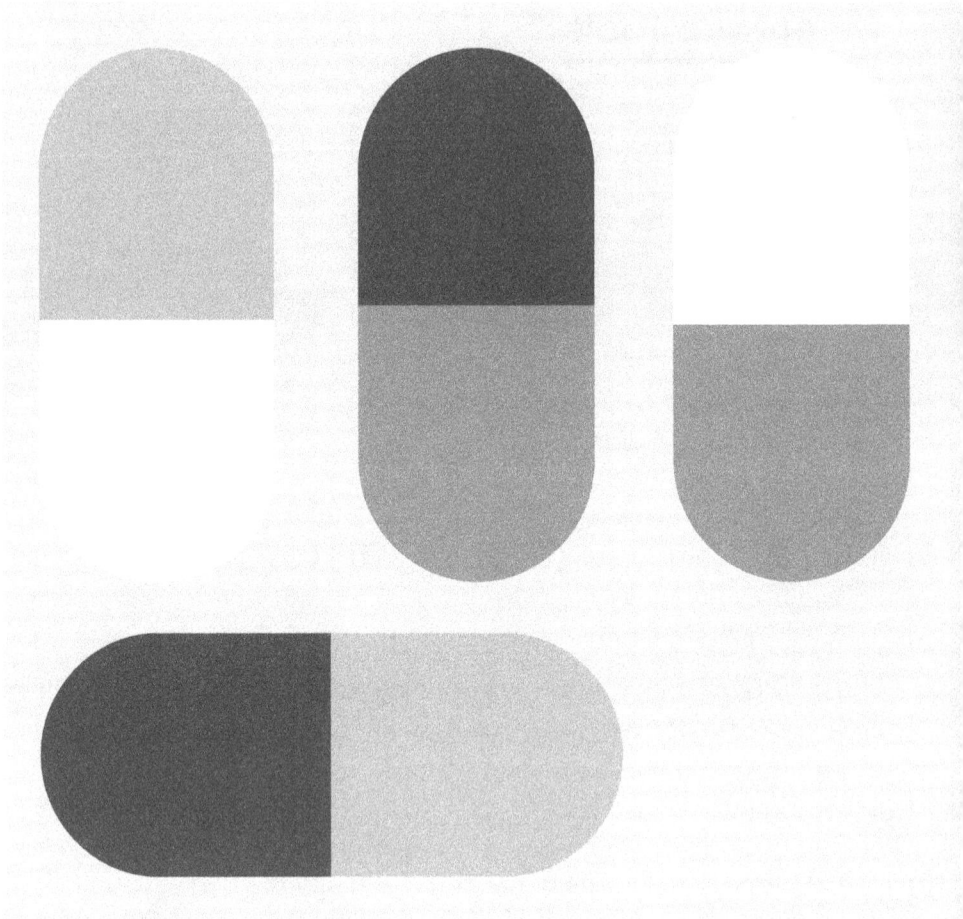

What it means to stretch myself is...

_____

_____

_____

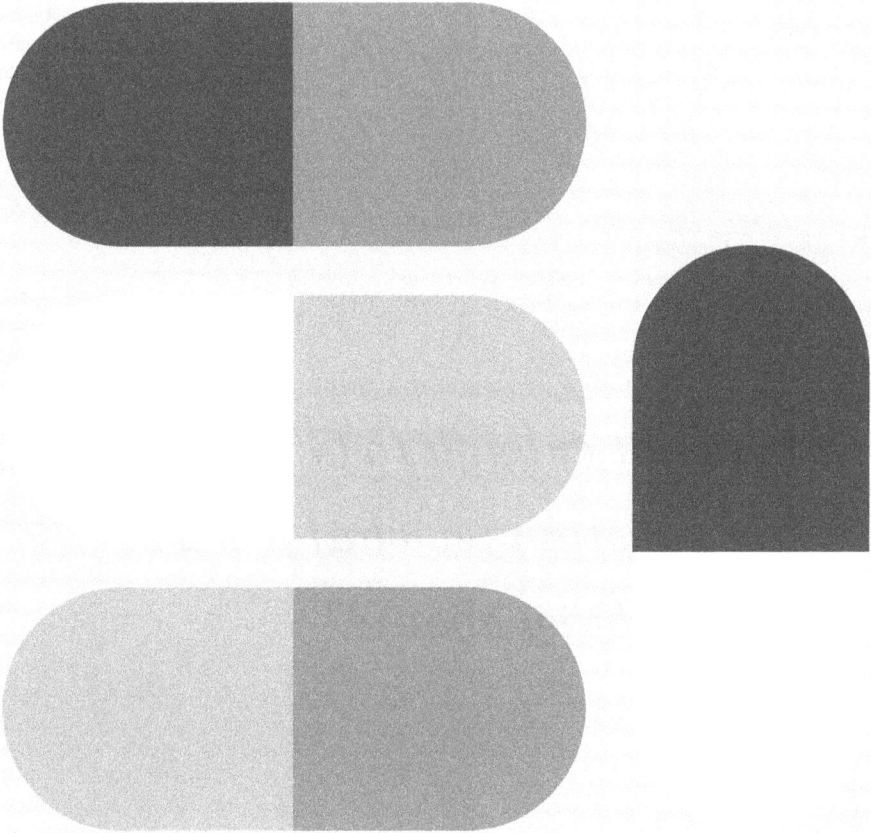

My Ambitions:

My Next 12 Months

"It is not enough to be busy... The question is: what are we busy about?"

HENRY DAVID THOREAU

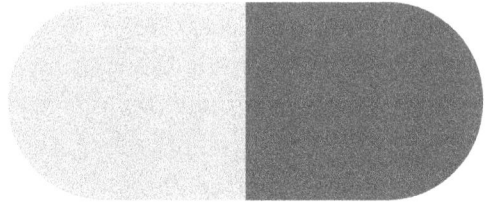

Let's start here. What do you envision for the next 12 months? What do you want to be busy about? If you're going to invest your time and effort, what does success look like for you?

In this section, we'll have you explore your ambitions and how you want to stretch yourself, setting your intentions for the year.

What's important is for you to look inside and ask yourself what YOU want. Because it will be hard to sustain your ambition if you're living someone else's agenda. The only way to make your life+work sustainable is to make the definition of success yours.

So what's next for you, on your terms? Explore broadly to start and then narrow down to what will hold your attention most in the coming 12 months.

Dream a little!

Use this space to illustrate your vision for the next 12 months. Draw inspirational pictures of what you want to have happen. Or, do a mind map that expresses key goals and what those mean to you. Create a collage of images that are inspirational to you. Anything goes. Use this space to envision your year.

Month/Year _____ to Month/Year _____

Deepen your understanding of your vision and your ambitions.
After visioning your year on the prior pages, further explore your ambitions with these prompts. Use those that inspire you to better understand yourself, your goals, and how you want to stretch yourself in the coming 12 months.

Month/Year _____ to Month/Year _____

I'll feel fulfilled this year if I...

_____

_____

I'll be thrilled this year if I...

_____

_____

Who I want to be this year is...

_____

_____

The ways I'd like to grow this year are...

_____

_____

The curiosities I'd like to explore this year are...

_____

_____

This year*...

I am committed to accomplishing...

_____

_____

_____

I am committed to achieving...

_____

_____

_____

I am determined to be...

_____

_____

_____

I am determined to contribute...

_____

_____

_____

I am determined to add value or offer...

_____

_____

_____

Focus and honesty help. Sustainable Ambition holds two opposing elements in tension—stretch and sustain. That means it's helpful to be clear on where you need and want to focus your attention in the coming 12 months.

Where I want to put attention in the next 12 months is...

_____

_____

_____

My stage in life means for my life+work I need to...

_____

_____

That means I'm going to put my focus on: _____ % Life / _____ % Work

In the coming year, the pace I want to be operating at is:

_____

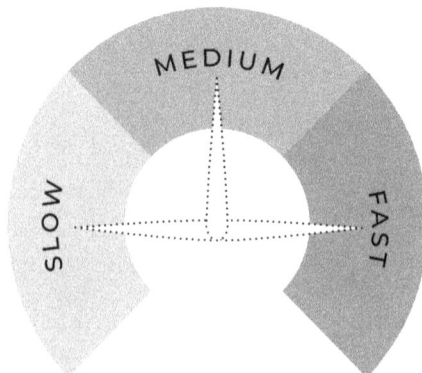

Other areas of my life that will need prioritized attention are*...

_____

_____

_____

_____

_____

_____

_____

_____

_____

_____

_____

_____

_____

_____

_____

_____

_____

Consider different dimensions, yet prioritize and simplify: career/vocation; family, community, and relationships; health; financial; growth and learning; fun and recreation; life+work resilience.

Set your ambitions. After visioning your year, exploring your ambitions, and understanding your focus, take the time now to summarize what you have learned. How do you want to stretch yourself? What are your ambitions and how will you define success?

Across my professional and personal life*, my ambitions for the next 12 months are: (circle one: good, very good, the best)

I want to be good / very good / the best at:

_____

I want to be good / very good / the best at:

_____

I want to be good / very good / the best at:

_____

I want to be good / very good / the best at:

_____

"Keep away from those who try to belittle your ambitions.
Small people always do that, but the really great make you
believe that you too can become great."

_____
MARK TWAIN

Define your own success*

Personal success for me this year looks like...

_____

_____

_____

I'll measure my personal success by...

_____

_____

_____

Professional success for me this year looks like...

_____

_____

_____

I'll measure my professional success by...

_____

_____

_____

*Consider different dimensions, yet prioritize and simplify: career/vocation; family, community, and relationships; health; financial; growth and learning; fun and recreation; life+work resilience.

Set your intentions for the year.

Knowing your ambitions and how you'll define success, now articulate a personal and professional purpose for the coming 12 months and note your priorities.

Personal Purpose

My purpose for this year will be to [what you want to do] by/through [how you'll do it] so that [your why: what impact you hope to make].

_____

_____

_____

_____

_____

_____

_____

_____

_____

_____

_____

_____

_____

_____

Professional Purpose

My purpose for this year will be to [what you want to do] by/through [how you'll do it] so that [your why: what impact you hope to make].

_____

_____

_____

_____

_____

_____

_____

_____

_____

_____

_____

_____

_____

_____

_____

_____

Example: My purpose is to be an empathic leader through listening more than speaking, coaching employees' gifts, and championing their ability to be and do more, so that everyone thrives and stretches to reach their potential.

The reality is we can't do it all. Now simplify down. What are your focused priorities* for the coming year?

My top 3 priorities for my personal life:

1. _____

2. _____

3. _____

My top 3 priorities for my professional life:

1. _____

2. _____

3. _____

Consider different dimensions, yet prioritize and simplify: career/vocation; family, community, and relationships; health; financial; growth and learning; fun and recreation; life+work resilience.

"Action expresses priorities."

GANDHI

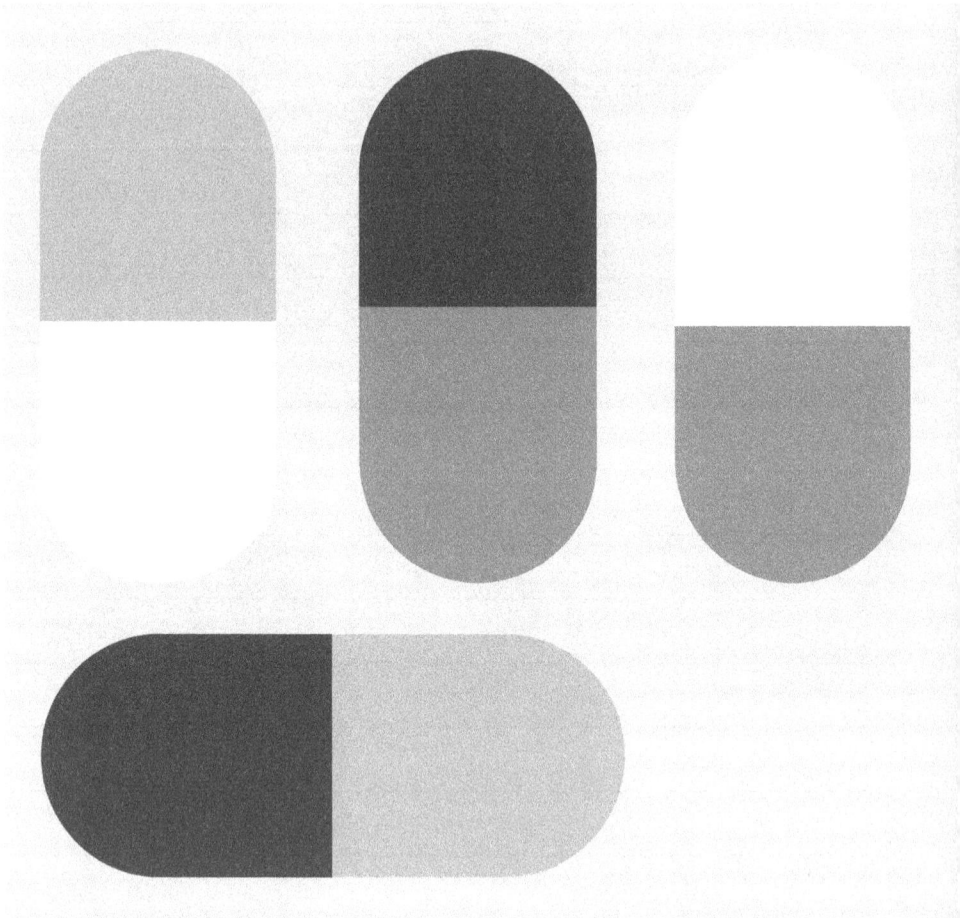

What it means to sustain myself is...

_____

_____

_____

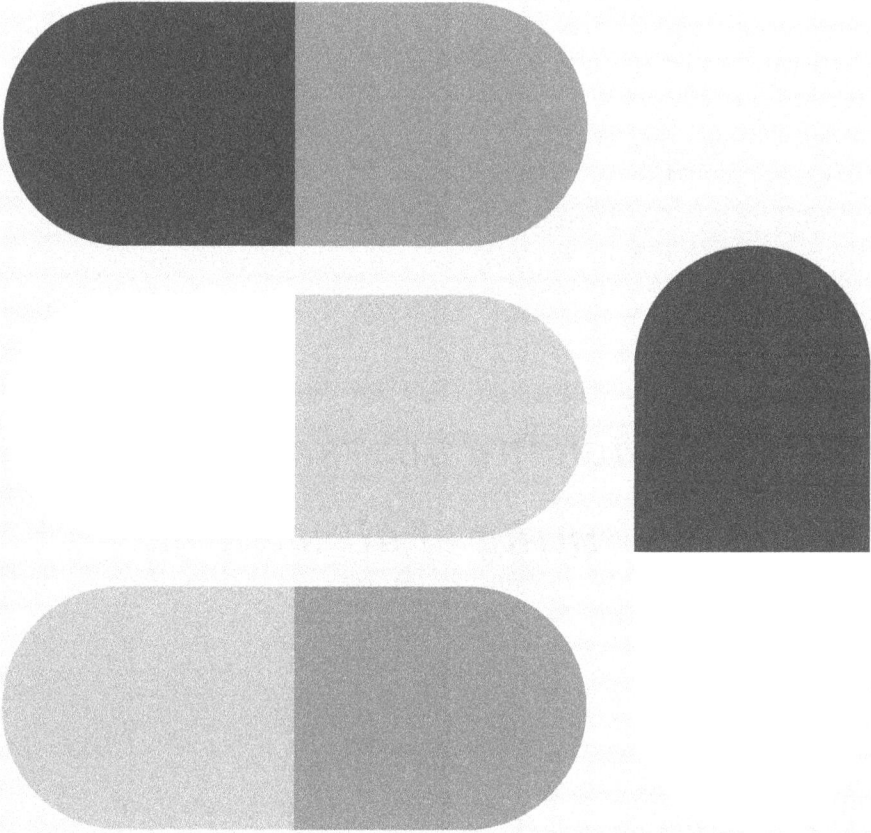

My Sustainable:

My Life+Work

Resilience Rx

"*Knowing yourself*
is the beginning of all wisdom."

ARISTOTLE

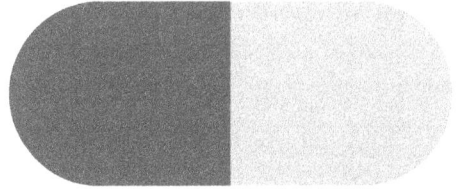

It's easy to fall into life and work running you vs. you running your life and work. So how do you start to take back control of your life+work and make it more sustainable?

It starts with tuning into yourself. What do you value? How do you best operate? What do you need to sustain yourself to keep you operating at your best each day?

And because your required effort is likely to ebb and flow over time, it's also important that you build resilience to sustain yourself over time.

When it comes to finding a cure for busyness, there is no one-size-fits-all approach. It needs to be self-defined. We are not all wired the same. You need to determine what works for you and write your own Life+Work Resilience Rx. And you might learn that prescription needs to change over time. It's not static.

But first, let's start with gaining insights about what you know about yourself now and how you operate at your best.

What do you value in your life?

These are elements that are core to you, your cornerstones. They reflect what is important to you or what drives and motivates you. Start by articulating the value, then probe deeper answering the following prompts. Better understanding what you value will help you prioritize what you need in your life+work to feel fulfilled and energized.

Value	I am someone who appreciates...
Growth & Learning	Always being on a growth curve and learning new concepts I can apply to my life and work

What this value looks like in my life is...	This is important to me, because...
Taking classes, reading fiction and non-fiction, listening to webinars, attending talks, going to museums	I want to better myself, and I get a lot of personal satisfaction and joy from learning

Get to know yourself better.

These 10 Insight Inquiries help you better understand how you tick and best operate. Your responses will help you craft your Life+Work Resilience Rx and be helpful reference as you go through your days.

Month/Year _____ to Month/Year _____

1. I get energized when...

_____

_____

_____

_____

_____

2. I get drained when...

_____

_____

_____

_____

_____

3. I get refueled and recover when...

_____

_____

_____

_____

_____

4. I really have fun and enjoy when...

_____

_____

_____

_____

_____

5. I know my boundaries have been crossed when...

_____

_____

_____

_____

_____

6. I do my best work when...

_____

_____

_____

_____

_____

_____

7. I am most in flow when...

_____

_____

_____

_____

_____

_____

8. I function at my best when the hour is...

morning   afternoon   night

9. I feel supported when...

_____

_____

_____

_____

_____

_____

_____

_____

_____

10. I feel like my life+work is sustainable when...

_____

_____

_____

_____

_____

_____

_____

_____

_____

_____

If we're going to stretch ourselves, we need to plan activities to sustain ourselves. What are the activities you need to do daily, weekly, monthly, quarterly and yearly to sustain yourself so you'll show up at your best?

Day	15 min meditation or workout	
Week	Date night with partner	
Month	Family weekend activity	
Quarter	Event with extended family	
Year	2 weeks off end of year	

Pauses and breaks are important. How do you like to take pauses during your days, weeks, months, quarters, or year? Pauses don't have to be long—they can be as short as taking 5 deep breaths or reciting a poem or going for a 15 minute walk. What types of breaks and pauses will help keep you sustained? You might find overlap with some of your sustaining activities, too.

Day	5 deep breaths at the top of each hour during the work day	
Week	At least 1 hour walk by myself	
Month	One full day for my creative work	
Quarter	A day hike with my friends	
Year	2 weeks off end of year	

To operate at my best, I prescribe...

My treatment:

I'm going to honor my values doing...

_____

_____

_____

_____

I am going to say yes to...

_____

_____

_____

_____

I will create these habits to support me working my best...

_____

_____

_____

_____

Take with + Frequency:

I will have fun by...

_____

_____

_____

_____

_____

I'm going to add these energizers...

_____

_____

_____

_____

_____

I will create these rituals for recovery...

_____

_____

_____

_____

_____

Refill:

I am also going to sustain myself by...

_____

_____

_____

I am going to give myself grace and allow myself to be bad at...

_____

_____

_____

Contraindications:

I am going to say no to...

_____

_____

_____

I'm going to eliminate these drainers ...

_____

_____

_____

Extra Strength:

The structures I'm going to put in place at work to support me are...

_____

_____

_____

The structures I'm going to put in place at home to support me are...

_____

_____

_____

The people in my life I need to get buy-in from are...

_____

_____

_____

The people I will enlist to support me are...

_____

_____

Reference your Life+Work Resilience Rx as you move forward into Planning each Quarter, Month, Week, and Day.

Make a commitment to yourself.

This year:

I am choosing...

_____

_____

_____

I will challenge myself to...

_____

_____

_____

I will make these requests...

_____

_____

_____

"Commitment is what transforms a promise into a reality."

ABRAHAM LINCOLN

My pledge for Sustainable Ambition and life+work resilience.

I pledge to remain committed to creating life+work resilience to support my Sustainable Ambition. That means I'll utilize my Rx and stay committed to planning, practicing, and progressing, taking small and big steps to learn what works best for me.

I also pledge to

_____

_____

_____

_____

_____

_____

_____

_____

_____

_____

_____

_____

Signature

The mantras that will keep me motivated are:

> 66
>
>   I'm committed to building my life+work resilience.

> 66

> 66

> 66

> 66

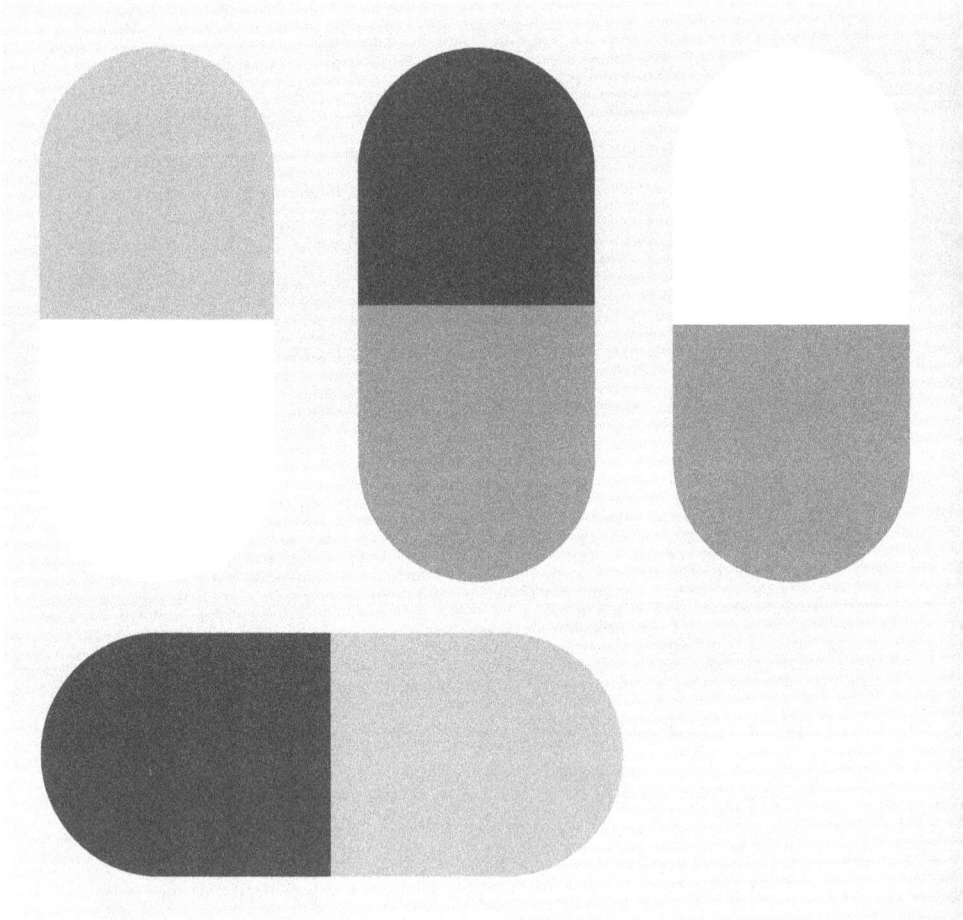

My next 12 months will be...

_____

_____

_____

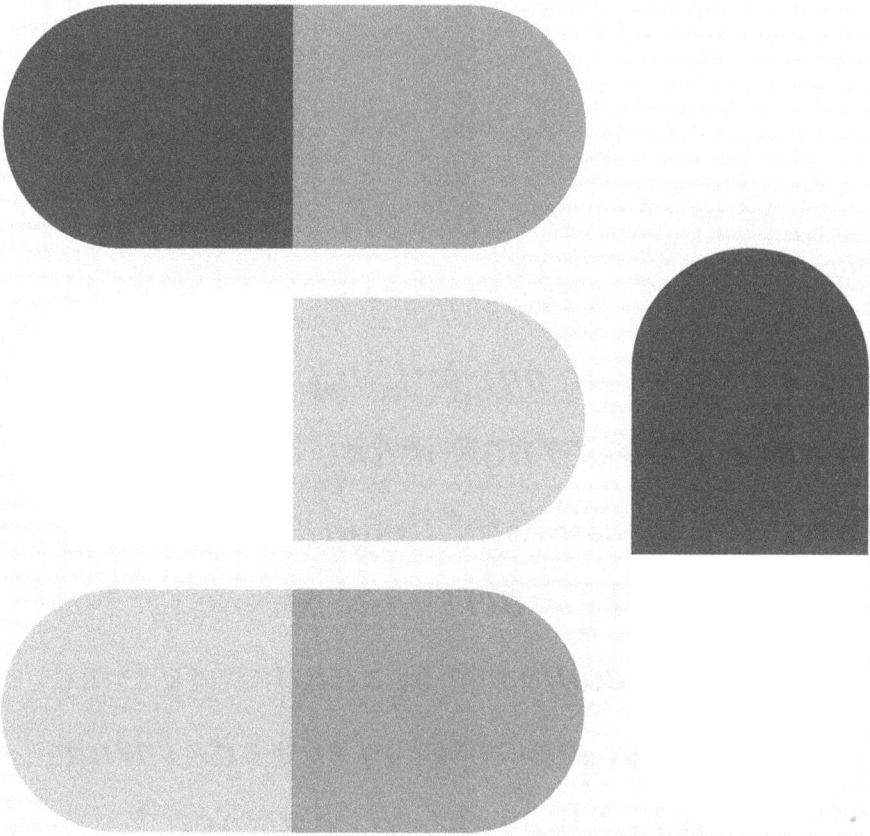

My 12-Month Planner

+ 6-Month Horizon

"You will find no one willing to share out his money; but to how many does each of us divide up his life! People are frugal in guarding their personal property; but as soon as it comes to squandering time they are most wasteful of the one thing in which it is right to be stingy."

SENECA

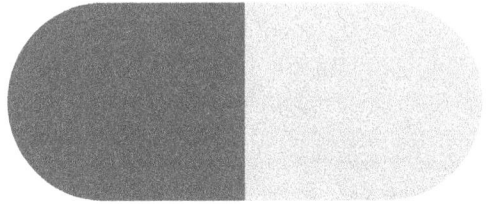

Planning your time is a must, otherwise others will control your calendar. Plus, unrealistic expectations can be a killer; they set us up for disappointment.

And, again, I hate to break it to you, but the reality is we likely won't experience "balance" all the time in every day, week, or month. What helps is to look to build sustainability over a longer time horizon. To be sure, consider your pace, but there may be times when you need to invest more effort and time given your ambitions, and there may be times that offer a bit more slack when you can recover and build back up your resilience stores.

So, let's take a look at your high-level plan and calendar for the next 12-months, and then look another 6 months out.

Let's start to map out the next 12 months. Given your vision and ambitions from Section 1, what are the core activities and projects that will need your attention over time to reach your end goals? Use this space to map a high-level action plan. Start with the end of year vision and then map backwards the high-level actions that need to be completed on the different time horizons.

Month/Year _____ to Month/Year _____

End Vision	12 months	9 months

6 months	3 months	1 month

Now let's plan your calendar. Look back to your vision, ambitions, and values—what do you need to put on your calendar to achieve your goals? What do you need to put on the calendar first to support your Life+Work Resilience Rx?

Month/Year _____ **to Month/Year** _____

Month/Year	Month/Year	Month/Year

Month/Year	Month/Year	Month/Year

Then fill in the other activities and events that are already planned for the coming 12 months across your personal and professional life. You may want to do this in pencil. If this is too small, consider a poster board and use post-it notes to plan elements of your year.

Month/Year	Month/Year	Month/Year
Month/Year	Month/Year	Month/Year

Let's take a look at your calendar. What do you observe?

How sustainable does your 12-month plan look?

_____

_____

_____

_____

_____

Are there too many activities happening at one time?

_____

_____

_____

_____

_____

Can and should anything be shifted?

_____

_____

_____

_____

_____

Are there enough sustaining activities on your calendar?

_____

_____

_____

When will you schedule time for recovery and rejuvenation?

_____

_____

_____

_____

When will you schedule time for your value-related activities?

_____

_____

_____

_____

When is your schedule or work going to be demanding?

_____

_____

_____

_____

What support do you need during those times?

_____

_____

_____

_____

_____

What do you need to negotiate at work to ensure you achieve sustainability over the year?

_____

_____

_____

_____

_____

What do you need to negotiate at home to ensure you achieve sustainability over the year?

_____

_____

_____

_____

_____

Let's look at your next 6 month horizon. If your coming 12 months look full, how can the following 6 months (months 13-18) support sustainability? Where might you build in more of your Life+Work Resilience Rx given what the coming 12 months look like?

Month/Year _____ **to Month/Year** _____

Month/Year	Month/Year	Month/Year

Or, do you find yourself looking at the following 6 months and wonder where you might stretch yourself next? What plans do you want on your 6-month horizon?

Month/Year	Month/Year	Month/Year

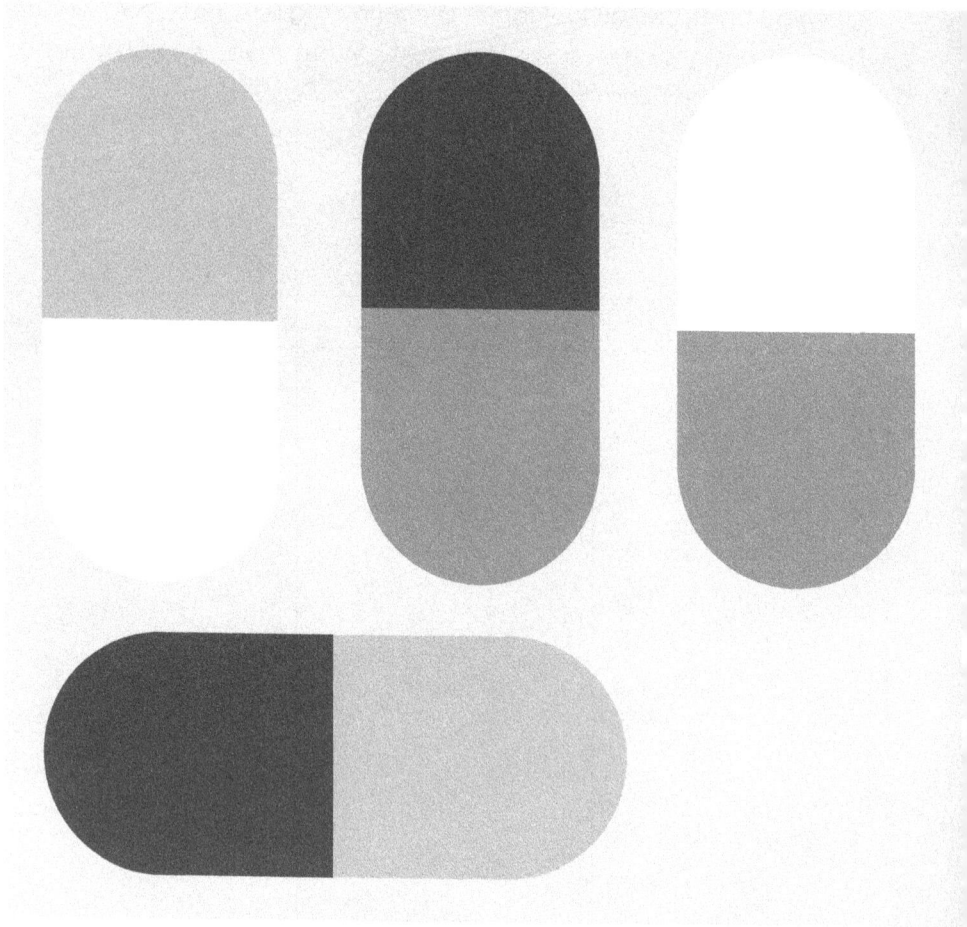

This quarter will be...

_____

_____

_____

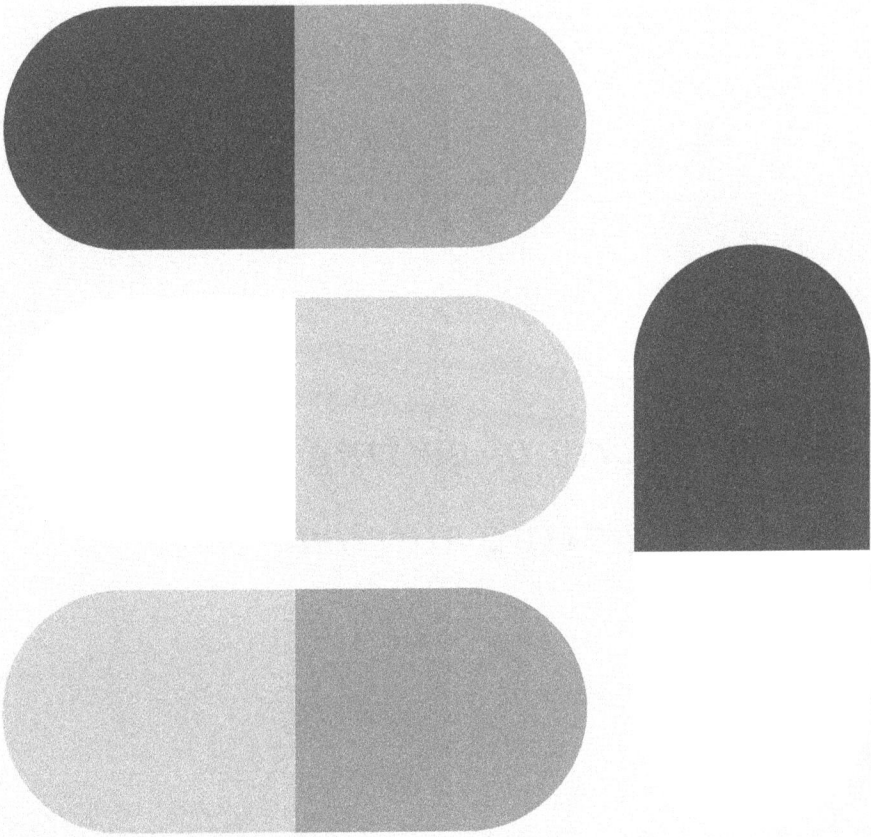

Quarter 1 + Months 1, 2, 3

Planner & Tracker

Aim, Act, Assess, Adapt

"The secret of getting ahead
is getting started."

MARK TWAIN

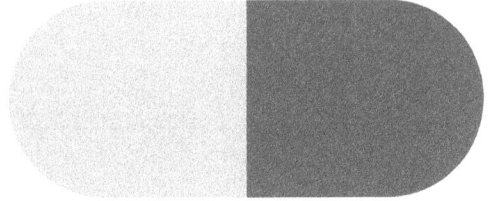

Creating Sustainable Ambition and building life+work resilience takes awareness and a bit of discipline. That's where the planner can help.

With the quarterly plans, it's time to aim and get into action, planning the next quarter, practicing, and tracking your progress. At the end of each month and then quarter, assess what's working and not working for you and determine how you'll adapt.

But first start by creating a Quarter Plan, Quarter Rx, and Monthly Plan, determining where you want to aim for the quarter and the activities that will stretch you and those that will sustain you over the three months. What's also important here is to get clear on actions or behaviors you'll want to try and practice.

Then, use the Month/Day tracker for awareness building and supporting your commitment to act and build your life+work resilience. Use the Month and Quarter Reviews to support your learning journey and progressing, assessing and adapting over time—what worked, what didn't, what's next? Put an appointment on your calendar now to check-in at the end of each month and the quarter.

Let's start to take back control of your life+work and make it more sustainable!

What's your aim for the quarter? First look back to Section 1: My Ambitions to remind yourself how you want to stretch yourself. What do you need to act on this quarter given your ambitions? What will success this quarter look like both personally and professionally?

Ambitions	Success
	Personal
	Professional

What's your focus for the quarter? What are your top 3 priorities across your personal and professional life? Also look back to Section 3: My 12-Month Planner and consider what from your calendar is important to note that will require your attention.

Top 3 Priorities	Calendar Notes
Personal	
Professional	

How will you sustain yourself this quarter? Review from Section 2 your Life+Work Resilience Rx. For the left page here, review sections: My Treatment, Take With, and Refill. For the next page, review sections Contraindications and Extra Strength.

QUARTER 1 - Months _____ , _____ , _____	
Value Activities	
Energizing Activities	
Sustaining Activities	
Pauses & Breaks	

Consider different elements of your Rx: ways to live your values, setting boundaries, new habits and rituals, sustaining activities, addressing energizers

Given what you're trying to achieve and how you'll stretch yourself this quarter, fill in the sections below to aim your quarter in the right direction to make it sustainable. Remember that we won't always have balance, so consider how you will support yourself to show up at your best.

QUARTER 1 - Months _____ , _____ , _____	
Boundaries	
Structures	
Support	
Try & Practice	

and drainers, productivity hacks or behaviors, making time for fun, or work and home structure to support your life+work resilience.

What's your aim for each month? Based on your Quarter Plan and Quarter Rx, now break down the important actions and activities for each month in the quarter. Make note of anything important on your calendar and what you expect your pace to be to plan accordingly.

	Month 1:
Ambition: Prioritized Actions	
Rx: Prioritized Activities	
Calendar Notes	
Pace	
Other Notes	

Month 2:	Month 3:

What are your actions? Use the Month/Day tracker for awareness building and supporting your commitment to act and build your life+work resilience. Each day, quickly run through and put a check mark by day in the boxes that are relevant for you. Over the month, what do you notice?

Month 1:	1	2	3	4	5	6	7	8	9	10	11	12
My Best Self: I was able to operate at my best today												
Energy: My energy level was good today												
Focus: I was focused on the right activities in alignment with my priorities												
Boundaries: I set boundaries today												
Sustain: I did something to sustain myself												
Pause: I took a pause or break today												
Practice: I practiced what I said I'd test out												
Grace: I gave myself or someone else grace												
Bad At: I allowed myself to be bad at something												
Support: I asked for support or help												

13	14	15	16	17	18	19	20	21	22	23	24	25	26	27	28	29	30	31

Month 2:	1	2	3	4	5	6	7	8	9	10	11	12
My Best Self: I was able to operate at my best today												
Energy: My energy level was good today												
Focus: I was focused on the right activities in alignment with my priorities												
Boundaries: I set boundaries today												
Sustain: I did something to sustain myself												
Pause: I took a pause or break today												
Practice: I practiced what I said I'd test out												
Grace: I gave myself or someone else grace												
Bad At: I allowed myself to be bad at something												
Support: I asked for support or help												

13	14	15	16	17	18	19	20	21	22	23	24	25	26	27	28	29	30	31

Month 3:	1	2	3	4	5	6	7	8	9	10	11	12
My Best Self: I was able to operate at my best today												
Energy: My energy level was good today												
Focus: I was focused on the right activities in alignment with my priorities												
Boundaries: I set boundaries today												
Sustain: I did something to sustain myself												
Pause: I took a pause or break today												
Practice: I practiced what I said I'd test out												
Grace: I gave myself or someone else grace												
Bad At: I allowed myself to be bad at something												
Support: I asked for support or help												

13	14	15	16	17	18	19	20	21	22	23	24	25	26	27	28	29	30	31

How is it going? At the end of each month, fill in the Month Review to track your progress, assessing how you are doing and determining how to adapt along the way.

Month 1: _____

What's working? What's not working?

How would you rate the following dimensions with 1 = low and 5 = high?

Life Satisfaction

1 □   2 □   3 □   4 □   5 □

Work Satisfaction

1 □   2 □   3 □   4 □   5 □

Sustainable

1 □   2 □   3 □   4 □   5 □

Ambition

1 □   2 □   3 □   4 □   5 □

Values

1 □   2 □   3 □   4 □   5 □

Priorities

1 □   2 □   3 □   4 □   5 □

Pace

1 □   2 □   3 □   4 □   5 □

Resilience

1 □   2 □   3 □   4 □   5 □

Energy

1 □   2 □   3 □   4 □   5 □

Productivity

1 □   2 □   3 □   4 □   5 □

Work Structures

1 □   2 □   3 □   4 □   5 □

Life Structures

1 □   2 □   3 □   4 □   5 □

What have I learned?

_____

_____

_____

_____

Month 2: _____

What's working? What's not working?

How would you rate the following dimensions with 1 = low and 5 = high?

Life Satisfaction
1 ▢   2 ▢   3 ▢   4 ▢   5 ▢

Pace
1 ▢   2 ▢   3 ▢   4 ▢   5 ▢

Work Satisfaction
1 ▢   2 ▢   3 ▢   4 ▢   5 ▢

Resilience
1 ▢   2 ▢   3 ▢   4 ▢   5 ▢

Sustainable
1 ▢   2 ▢   3 ▢   4 ▢   5 ▢

Energy
1 ▢   2 ▢   3 ▢   4 ▢   5 ▢

Ambition
1 ▢   2 ▢   3 ▢   4 ▢   5 ▢

Productivity
1 ▢   2 ▢   3 ▢   4 ▢   5 ▢

Values
1 ▢   2 ▢   3 ▢   4 ▢   5 ▢

Work Structures
1 ▢   2 ▢   3 ▢   4 ▢   5 ▢

Priorities
1 ▢   2 ▢   3 ▢   4 ▢   5 ▢

Life Structures
1 ▢   2 ▢   3 ▢   4 ▢   5 ▢

What have I learned?

_____

_____

_____

_____

_____

_____

_____

Month 3: _____

What's working? What's not working?

How would you rate the following dimensions with 1 = low and 5 = high?

Life Satisfaction
1 □   2 □   3 □   4 □   5 □

Pace
1 □   2 □   3 □   4 □   5 □

Work Satisfaction
1 □   2 □   3 □   4 □   5 □

Resilience
1 □   2 □   3 □   4 □   5 □

Sustainable
1 □   2 □   3 □   4 □   5 □

Energy
1 □   2 □   3 □   4 □   5 □

Ambition
1 □   2 □   3 □   4 □   5 □

Productivity
1 □   2 □   3 □   4 □   5 □

Values
1 □   2 □   3 □   4 □   5 □

Work Structures
1 □   2 □   3 □   4 □   5 □

Priorities
1 □   2 □   3 □   4 □   5 □

Life Structures
1 □   2 □   3 □   4 □   5 □

What have I learned?

_____

_____

_____

_____

_____

_____

_____

_____

How did it go? At the end of the quarter, fill in the Quarter Review to assess how the quarter went and to identify opportunities to adapt next quarter.

Quarter 1: _____

What's working? What's not working?

How would you rate the following dimensions with 1 = low and 5 = high?

Life Satisfaction
1 □   2 □   3 □   4 □   5 □

Pace
1 □   2 □   3 □   4 □   5 □

Work Satisfaction
1 □   2 □   3 □   4 □   5 □

Resilience
1 □   2 □   3 □   4 □   5 □

Sustainable
1 □   2 □   3 □   4 □   5 □

Energy
1 □   2 □   3 □   4 □   5 □

Ambition
1 □   2 □   3 □   4 □   5 □

Productivity
1 □   2 □   3 □   4 □   5 □

Values
1 □   2 □   3 □   4 □   5 □

Work Structures
1 □   2 □   3 □   4 □   5 □

Priorities
1 □   2 □   3 □   4 □   5 □

Life Structures
1 □   2 □   3 □   4 □   5 □

What have I learned?

_____

_____

_____

_____

What worked?

_____

_____

_____

_____

What didn't work?

_____

_____

_____

_____

What was unsustainable?

_____

_____

_____

_____

What do you want to do differently next quarter?

_____

_____

_____

_____

What I've learned about myself...

_____

_____

_____

New boundaries I want to set are...

_____

_____

_____

New work structures I want to set are...

_____

_____

_____

New home structures I want to set are...

_____

_____

_____

What I also want to try and practice next are...

_____

_____

_____

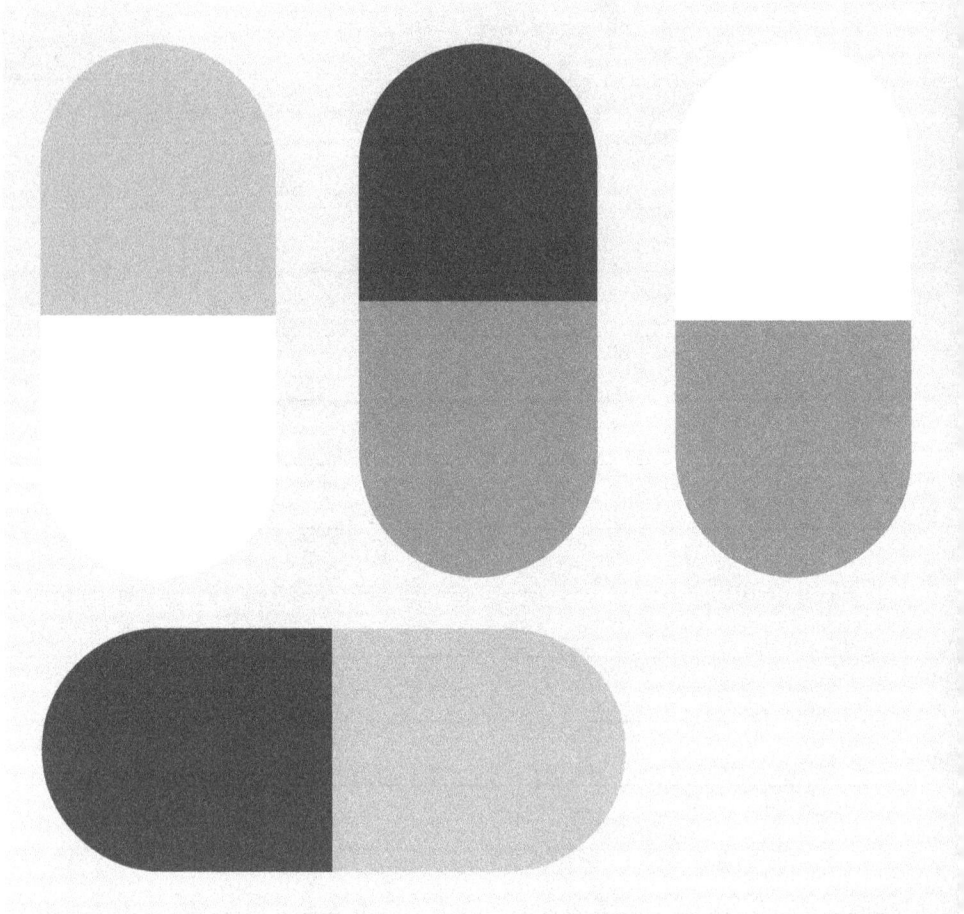

This quarter will be...

_____

_____

_____

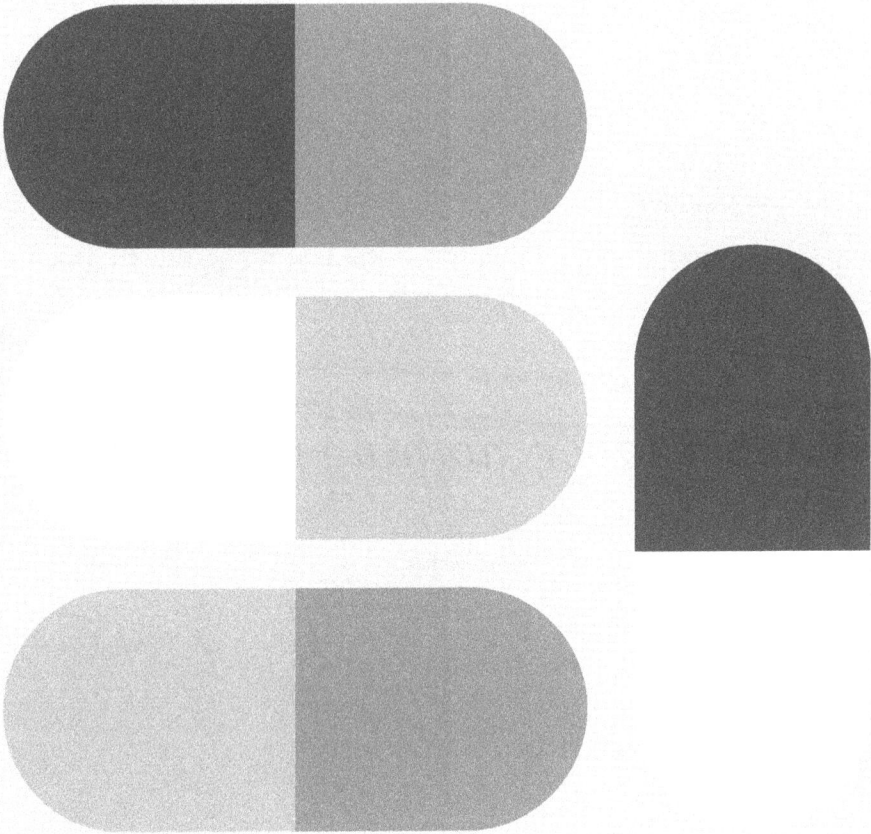

Quarter 2 + Months 4, 5, 6

Planner & Tracker

Aim, Act, Assess, Adapt

"Without labor, nothing prospers."

SOPHOCLES

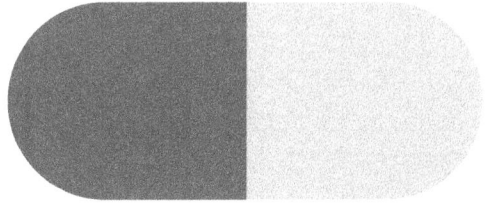

Let's do it again! Start by going back to your ambitions for these 12 months, your Life+Work Resilience Rx, and your 12-Month Planner. Remind yourself about your vision for the year, what success looks like, and your intentions. What was important to focus on, and how do you want to build resilience? From there, you'll map out the next quarter. What is your aim? What's on the horizon for the next 3 months?

Also review the last quarter. Pull forward the learning and what you want to try and practice next.

Remember, creating Sustainable Ambition and building life+work resilience takes awareness and a bit of discipline. And the planner is here to support you.

Plan the next quarter, practice, and track your progress. At the end of each month and then quarter, assess what's working and not working for you and determine how you'll adapt. Put an appointment on your calendar now to check-in at the end of each month and the quarter.

What's your aim for the quarter? First look back to Section 1: My Ambitions to remind yourself how you want to stretch yourself. What do you need to act on this quarter given your ambitions? What will success this quarter look like both personally and professionally?

Ambitions	Success
	Personal
	Professional

What's your focus for the quarter? What are your top 3 priorities across your personal and professional life? Also look back to Section 3: My 12-Month Planner and consider what from your calendar is important to note that will require your attention.

Top 3 Priorities	Calendar Notes
Personal	
Professional	

How will you sustain yourself this quarter? Review from Section 2 your Life+Work Resilience Rx. For the left page here, review sections: My Treatment, Take With, and Refill. For the next page, review sections Contraindications and Extra Strength.

QUARTER 2 - Months _____ , _____ , _____	
Value Activities	
Energizing Activities	
Sustaining Activities	
Pauses & Breaks	

*Consider different elements of your Rx: ways to live your values, setting boundaries, new habits and rituals, sustaining activities, addressing energizers

Given what you're trying to achieve and how you'll stretch yourself this quarter, fill in the sections below to aim your quarter in the right direction to make it sustainable. Remember that we won't always have balance, so consider how you will support yourself to show up at your best.

QUARTER 2 - Months _____ , _____ , _____	
Boundaries	
Structures	
Support	
Try & Practice	

and drainers, productivity hacks or behaviors, making time for fun, or work and home structure to support your life+work resilience.

What's your aim for each month? Based on your Quarter Plan and Quarter Rx, now break down the important actions and activities for each month in the quarter. Make note of anything important on your calendar and what you expect your pace to be to plan accordingly.

	Month 4:
Ambition: Prioritized Actions	
Rx: Prioritized Activities	
Calendar Notes	
Pace	
Other Notes	

Month 5:	Month 6:

What are your actions? Use the Month/Day tracker for awareness building and supporting your commitment to act and build your life+work resilience. Each day, quickly run through and put a check mark by day in the boxes that are relevant for you. Over the month, what do you notice?

Month 4:	1	2	3	4	5	6	7	8	9	10	11	12
My Best Self: I was able to operate at my best today												
Energy: My energy level was good today												
Focus: I was focused on the right activities in alignment with my priorities												
Boundaries: I set boundaries today												
Sustain: I did something to sustain myself												
Pause: I took a pause or break today												
Practice: I practiced what I said I'd test out												
Grace: I gave myself or someone else grace												
Bad At: I allowed myself to be bad at something												
Support: I asked for support or help												

13	14	15	16	17	18	19	20	21	22	23	24	25	26	27	28	29	30	31

Month 5:	1	2	3	4	5	6	7	8	9	10	11	1:
My Best Self: I was able to operate at my best today												
Energy: My energy level was good today												
Focus: I was focused on the right activities in alignment with my priorities												
Boundaries: I set boundaries today												
Sustain: I did something to sustain myself												
Pause: I took a pause or break today												
Practice: I practiced what I said I'd test out												
Grace: I gave myself or someone else grace												
Bad At: I allowed myself to be bad at something												
Support: I asked for support or help												

13	14	15	16	17	18	19	20	21	22	23	24	25	26	27	28	29	30	31

Month 6:	1	2	3	4	5	6	7	8	9	10	11	12
My Best Self: I was able to operate at my best today												
Energy: My energy level was good today												
Focus: I was focused on the right activities in alignment with my priorities												
Boundaries: I set boundaries today												
Sustain: I did something to sustain myself												
Pause: I took a pause or break today												
Practice: I practiced what I said I'd test out												
Grace: I gave myself or someone else grace												
Bad At: I allowed myself to be bad at something												
Support: I asked for support or help												

13	14	15	16	17	18	19	20	21	22	23	24	25	26	27	28	29	30	31

How is it going? At the end of each month, fill in the Month Review to track your progress, assessing how you are doing and determining how to adapt along the way.

Month 4: _____

What's working? What's not working?

How would you rate the following dimensions with 1 = low and 5 = high?

Life Satisfaction
1 □   2 □   3 □   4 □   5 □

Pace
1 □   2 □   3 □   4 □   5 □

Work Satisfaction
1 □   2 □   3 □   4 □   5 □

Resilience
1 □   2 □   3 □   4 □   5 □

Sustainable
1 □   2 □   3 □   4 □   5 □

Energy
1 □   2 □   3 □   4 □   5 □

Ambition
1 □   2 □   3 □   4 □   5 □

Productivity
1 □   2 □   3 □   4 □   5 □

Values
1 □   2 □   3 □   4 □   5 □

Work Structures
1 □   2 □   3 □   4 □   5 □

Priorities
1 □   2 □   3 □   4 □   5 □

Life Structures
1 □   2 □   3 □   4 □   5 □

What have I learned?

_____

_____

_____

_____

Month 5: _____

What's working? What's not working?

How would you rate the following dimensions with 1 = low and 5 = high?

Life Satisfaction
1 □   2 □   3 □   4 □   5 □

Pace
1 □   2 □   3 □   4 □   5 □

Work Satisfaction
1 □   2 □   3 □   4 □   5 □

Resilience
1 □   2 □   3 □   4 □   5 □

Sustainable
1 □   2 □   3 □   4 □   5 □

Energy
1 □   2 □   3 □   4 □   5 □

Ambition
1 □   2 □   3 □   4 □   5 □

Productivity
1 □   2 □   3 □   4 □   5 □

Values
1 □   2 □   3 □   4 □   5 □

Work Structures
1 □   2 □   3 □   4 □   5 □

Priorities
1 □   2 □   3 □   4 □   5 □

Life Structures
1 □   2 □   3 □   4 □   5 □

What have I learned?

_____

_____

_____

_____

_____

_____

_____

Month 6: _____

What's working? What's not working?

How would you rate the following dimensions with 1 = low and 5 = high?

Life Satisfaction
1 □   2 □   3 □   4 □   5 □

Pace
1 □   2 □   3 □   4 □   5 □

Work Satisfaction
1 □   2 □   3 □   4 □   5 □

Resilience
1 □   2 □   3 □   4 □   5 □

Sustainable
1 □   2 □   3 □   4 □   5 □

Energy
1 □   2 □   3 □   4 □   5 □

Ambition
1 □   2 □   3 □   4 □   5 □

Productivity
1 □   2 □   3 □   4 □   5 □

Values
1 □   2 □   3 □   4 □   5 □

Work Structures
1 □   2 □   3 □   4 □   5 □

Priorities
1 □   2 □   3 □   4 □   5 □

Life Structures
1 □   2 □   3 □   4 □   5 □

What have I learned?

_____

_____

_____

_____

_____

_____

_____

How did it go? At the end of the quarter, fill in the Quarter Review to assess how the quarter went and to identify opportunities to adapt next quarter.

Quarter 2: _____

What's working? What's not working?

How would you rate the following dimensions with 1 = low and 5 = high?

Life Satisfaction
1 □   2 □   3 □   4 □   5 □

Pace
1 □   2 □   3 □   4 □   5 □

Work Satisfaction
1 □   2 □   3 □   4 □   5 □

Resilience
1 □   2 □   3 □   4 □   5 □

Sustainable
1 □   2 □   3 □   4 □   5 □

Energy
1 □   2 □   3 □   4 □   5 □

Ambition
1 □   2 □   3 □   4 □   5 □

Productivity
1 □   2 □   3 □   4 □   5 □

Values
1 □   2 □   3 □   4 □   5 □

Work Structures
1 □   2 □   3 □   4 □   5 □

Priorities
1 □   2 □   3 □   4 □   5 □

Life Structures
1 □   2 □   3 □   4 □   5 □

What have I learned?

_____

_____

_____

_____

What worked?

_____

_____

_____

_____

What didn't work?

_____

_____

_____

_____

What was unsustainable?

_____

_____

_____

_____

What do you want to do differently next quarter?

_____

_____

_____

_____

What I've learned about myself...

_____

_____

_____

New boundaries I want to set are...

_____

_____

_____

New work structures I want to set are...

_____

_____

_____

New home structures I want to set are...

_____

_____

_____

What I also want to try and practice next are...

_____

_____

_____

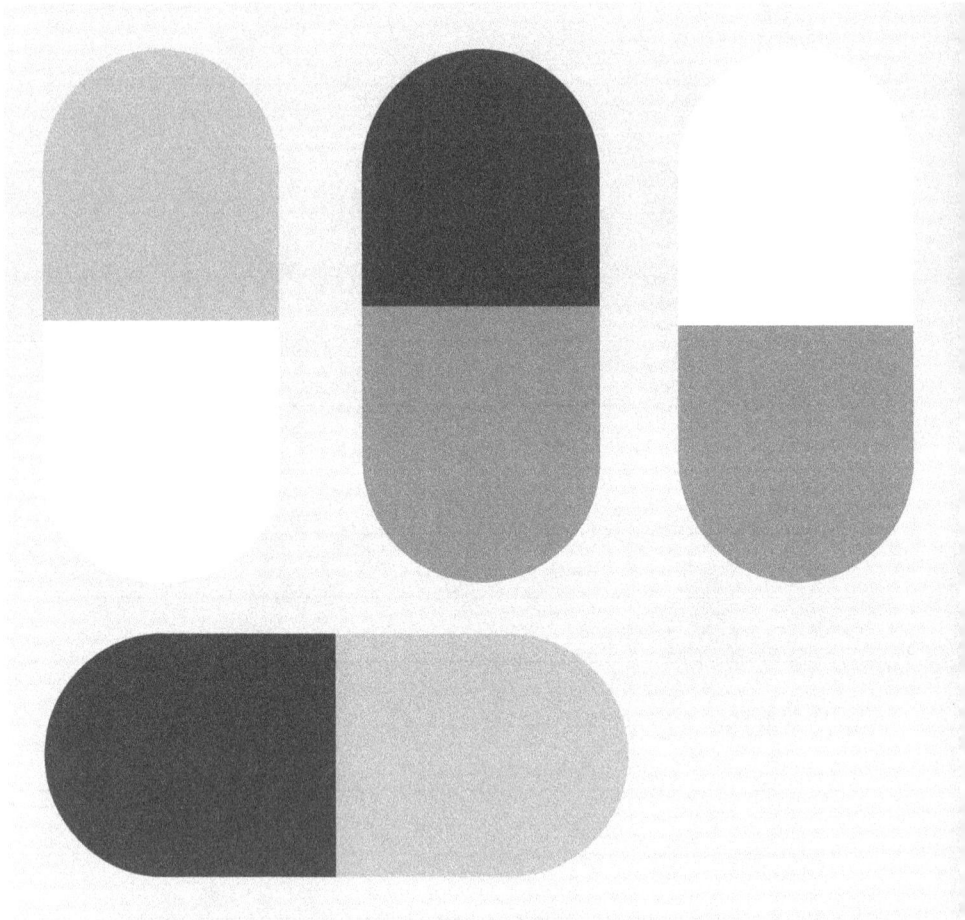

This quarter will be...

_____

_____

_____

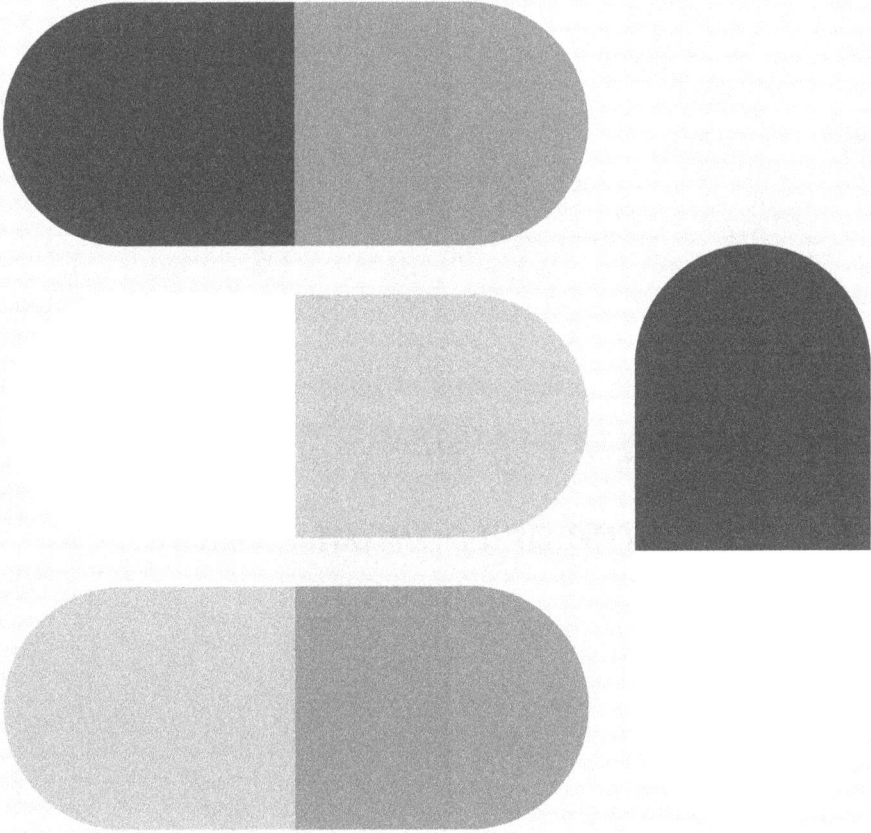

Quarter 3 + Months 7, 8, 9

Planner & Tracker

Aim, Act, Assess, Adapt

"I attribute my success to this:
I never gave or took an excuse."

FLORENCE NIGHTINGALE

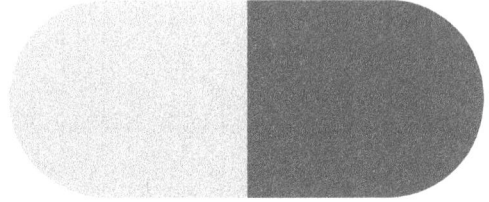

Here we go again! Start by going back to your ambitions for these 12 months, your Life+Work Resilience Rx, and your 12-Month Planner. Remind yourself about your vision for the year, what success looks like, and your intentions. What was important to focus on, and how do you want to build resilience? From there, you'll map out the next quarter. What is your aim? What's on the horizon for the next 3 months?

Also review the last quarter. Pull forward the learning and what you want to try and practice next.

Remember, creating Sustainable Ambition and building life+work resilience takes awareness and a bit of discipline. And the planner is here to support you.

Plan the next quarter, practice, and track your progress. At the end of each month and then quarter, assess what's working and not working for you and determine how you'll adapt. Put an appointment on your calendar now to check-in at the end of each month and the quarter.

What's your aim for the quarter? First look back to Section 1: My Ambitions to remind yourself how you want to stretch yourself. What do you need to act on this quarter given your ambitions? What will success this quarter look like both personally and professionally?

Ambitions	Success
	Personal
	Professional

What's your focus for the quarter? What are your top 3 priorities across your personal and professional life? Also look back to Section 3: My 12-Month Planner and consider what from your calendar is important to note that will require your attention.

Top 3 Priorities	Calendar Notes
Personal	
Professional	

How will you sustain yourself this quarter? Review from Section 2 your Life+Work Resilience Rx. For the left page here, review sections: My Treatment, Take With, and Refill. For the next page, review sections Contraindications and Extra Strength.

QUARTER 3 - Months _____ , _____ , _____	
Value Activities	
Energizing Activities	
Sustaining Activities	
Pauses & Breaks	

*Consider different elements of your Rx: ways to live your values, setting bound-aries, new habits and rituals, sustaining activities, addressing energizers

Given what you're trying to achieve and how you'll stretch yourself this quarter, fill in the sections below to aim your quarter in the right direction to make it sustainable. Remember that we won't always have balance, so consider how you will support yourself to show up at your best.

QUARTER 3 - Months _____ , _____ , _____	
Boundaries	
Structures	
Support	
Try & Practice	

and drainers, productivity hacks or behaviors, making time for fun, or work and home structure to support your life+work resilience.

What's your aim for each month? Based on your Quarter Plan and Quarter Rx, now break down the important actions and activities for each month in the quarter. Make note of anything important on your calendar and what you expect your pace to be to plan accordingly.

	Month 7:
Ambition: Prioritized Actions	
Rx: Prioritized Activities	
Calendar Notes	
Pace	
Other Notes	

Month 8:	Month 9:

What are your actions? Use the Month/Day tracker for awareness building and supporting your commitment to act and build your life+work resilience. Each day, quickly run through and put a check mark by day in the boxes that are relevant for you. Over the month, what do you notice?

Month 7:	1	2	3	4	5	6	7	8	9	10	11	12
My Best Self: I was able to operate at my best today												
Energy: My energy level was good today												
Focus: I was focused on the right activities in alignment with my priorities												
Boundaries: I set boundaries today												
Sustain: I did something to sustain myself												
Pause: I took a pause or break today												
Practice: I practiced what I said I'd test out												
Grace: I gave myself or someone else grace												
Bad At: I allowed myself to be bad at something												
Support: I asked for support or help												

13	14	15	16	17	18	19	20	21	22	23	24	25	26	27	28	29	30	31

Month 8:	1	2	3	4	5	6	7	8	9	10	11	12
My Best Self: I was able to operate at my best today												
Energy: My energy level was good today												
Focus: I was focused on the right activities in alignment with my priorities												
Boundaries: I set boundaries today												
Sustain: I did something to sustain myself												
Pause: I took a pause or break today												
Practice: I practiced what I said I'd test out												
Grace: I gave myself or someone else grace												
Bad At: I allowed myself to be bad at something												
Support: I asked for support or help												

13	14	15	16	17	18	19	20	21	22	23	24	25	26	27	28	29	30	31

Month 9:	1	2	3	4	5	6	7	8	9	10	11	12
My Best Self: I was able to operate at my best today												
Energy: My energy level was good today												
Focus: I was focused on the right activities in alignment with my priorities												
Boundaries: I set boundaries today												
Sustain: I did something to sustain myself												
Pause: I took a pause or break today												
Practice: I practiced what I said I'd test out												
Grace: I gave myself or someone else grace												
Bad At: I allowed myself to be bad at something												
Support: I asked for support or help												

13	14	15	16	17	18	19	20	21	22	23	24	25	26	27	28	29	30	31

How is it going? At the end of each month, fill in the Month Review to track your progress, assessing how you are doing and determining how to adapt along the way.

Month 7: _____

What's working? What's not working?

How would you rate the following dimensions with 1 = low and 5 = high?

Life Satisfaction					Pace				
1 □	2 □	3 □	4 □	5 □	1 □	2 □	3 □	4 □	5 □

Work Satisfaction					Resilience				
1 □	2 □	3 □	4 □	5 □	1 □	2 □	3 □	4 □	5 □

Sustainable					Energy				
1 □	2 □	3 □	4 □	5 □	1 □	2 □	3 □	4 □	5 □

Ambition					Productivity				
1 □	2 □	3 □	4 □	5 □	1 □	2 □	3 □	4 □	5 □

Values					Work Structures				
1 □	2 □	3 □	4 □	5 □	1 □	2 □	3 □	4 □	5 □

Priorities					Life Structures				
1 □	2 □	3 □	4 □	5 □	1 □	2 □	3 □	4 □	5 □

What have I learned?

_____

_____

_____

_____

Month 8: _____

What's working? What's not working?

How would you rate the following dimensions with 1 = low and 5 = high?

Life Satisfaction
1 ☐   2 ☐   3 ☐   4 ☐   5 ☐

Pace
1 ☐   2 ☐   3 ☐   4 ☐   5 ☐

Work Satisfaction
1 ☐   2 ☐   3 ☐   4 ☐   5 ☐

Resilience
1 ☐   2 ☐   3 ☐   4 ☐   5 ☐

Sustainable
1 ☐   2 ☐   3 ☐   4 ☐   5 ☐

Energy
1 ☐   2 ☐   3 ☐   4 ☐   5 ☐

Ambition
1 ☐   2 ☐   3 ☐   4 ☐   5 ☐

Productivity
1 ☐   2 ☐   3 ☐   4 ☐   5 ☐

Values
1 ☐   2 ☐   3 ☐   4 ☐   5 ☐

Work Structures
1 ☐   2 ☐   3 ☐   4 ☐   5 ☐

Priorities
1 ☐   2 ☐   3 ☐   4 ☐   5 ☐

Life Structures
1 ☐   2 ☐   3 ☐   4 ☐   5 ☐

What have I learned?

_____

_____

_____

_____

_____

_____

_____

Month 9: _____

What's working? What's not working?

How would you rate the following dimensions with 1 = low and 5 = high?

Life Satisfaction
1 □   2 □   3 □   4 □   5 □

Pace
1 □   2 □   3 □   4 □   5 □

Work Satisfaction
1 □   2 □   3 □   4 □   5 □

Resilience
1 □   2 □   3 □   4 □   5 □

Sustainable
1 □   2 □   3 □   4 □   5 □

Energy
1 □   2 □   3 □   4 □   5 □

Ambition
1 □   2 □   3 □   4 □   5 □

Productivity
1 □   2 □   3 □   4 □   5 □

Values
1 □   2 □   3 □   4 □   5 □

Work Structures
1 □   2 □   3 □   4 □   5 □

Priorities
1 □   2 □   3 □   4 □   5 □

Life Structures
1 □   2 □   3 □   4 □   5 □

What have I learned?

_____

_____

_____

_____

_____

_____

_____

How did it go? At the end of the quarter, fill in the Quarter Review to assess how the quarter went and to identify opportunities to adapt next quarter.

Quarter 3: _____

What's working? What's not working?

How would you rate the following dimensions with 1 = low and 5 = high?

Life Satisfaction
1 □   2 □   3 □   4 □   5 □

Pace
1 □   2 □   3 □   4 □   5 □

Work Satisfaction
1 □   2 □   3 □   4 □   5 □

Resilience
1 □   2 □   3 □   4 □   5 □

Sustainable
1 □   2 □   3 □   4 □   5 □

Energy
1 □   2 □   3 □   4 □   5 □

Ambition
1 □   2 □   3 □   4 □   5 □

Productivity
1 □   2 □   3 □   4 □   5 □

Values
1 □   2 □   3 □   4 □   5 □

Work Structures
1 □   2 □   3 □   4 □   5 □

Priorities
1 □   2 □   3 □   4 □   5 □

Life Structures
1 □   2 □   3 □   4 □   5 □

What have I learned?

_____

_____

_____

_____

What worked?

_____

_____

_____

_____

What didn't work?

_____

_____

_____

_____

What was unsustainable?

_____

_____

_____

_____

What do you want to do differently next quarter?

_____

_____

_____

_____

What I've learned about myself...

_____

_____

_____

New boundaries I want to set are...

_____

_____

_____

New work structures I want to set are...

_____

_____

_____

New home structures I want to set are...

_____

_____

_____

What I also want to try and practice next are...

_____

_____

_____

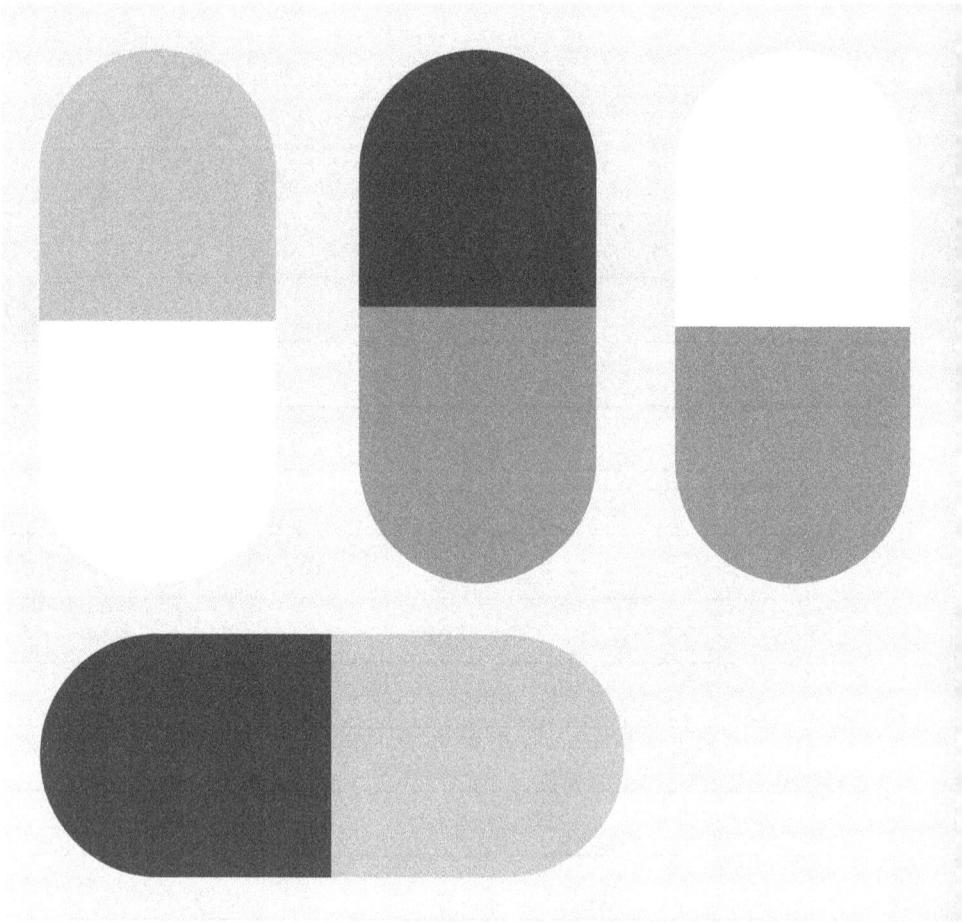

This quarter will be...

_____

_____

_____

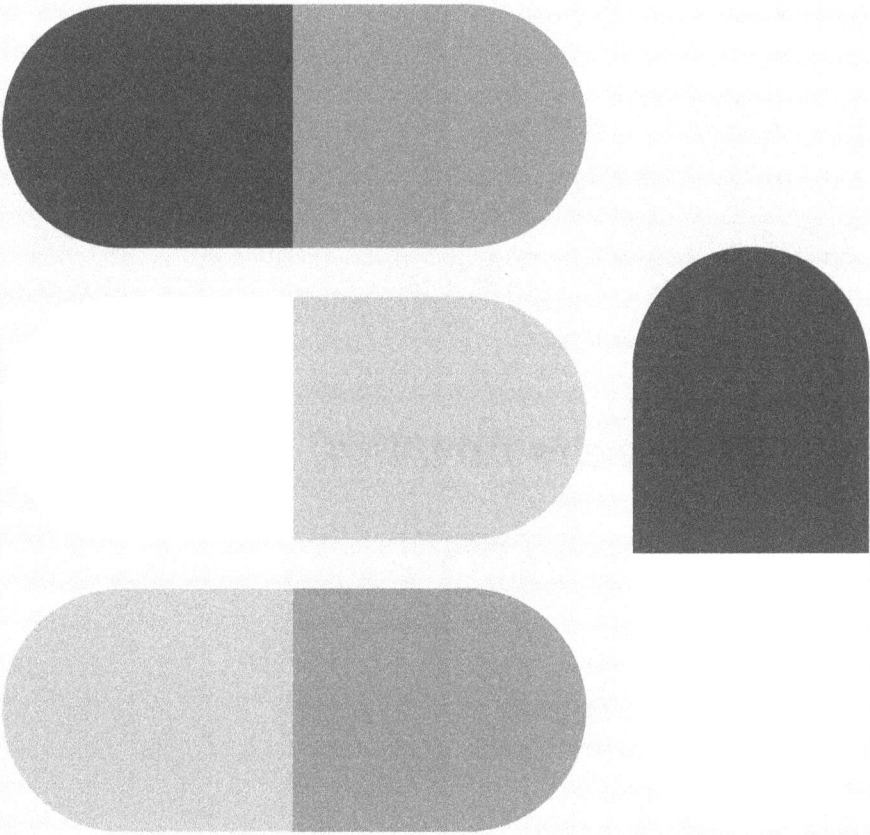

Quarter 4 + Months 10, 11, 12

Planner & Tracker

Aim, Act, Assess, Adapt

"If there is no wind, row."

MARK TWAIN

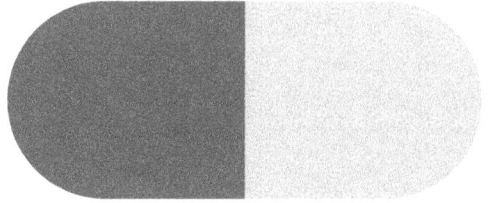

One more quarter! Start by going back to your ambitions for these 12 months, your Life+Work Resilience Rx, and your 12-Month Planner. Remind yourself about your vision for the year, what success looks like, and your intentions. What was important to focus on, and how do you want to build resilience? From there, you'll map out the next quarter. What is your aim? What's on the horizon for the next 3 months?

Also review the last quarter. Pull forward the learning and what you want to try and practice next.

Remember, creating Sustainable Ambition and building life+work resilience takes awareness and a bit of discipline. And the planner is here to support you.

Plan the next quarter, practice, and track your progress. At the end of each month and then quarter, assess what's working and not working for you and determine how you'll adapt. Put an appointment on your calendar now to check-in at the end of each month and the quarter.

What's your aim for the quarter? First look back to Section 1: My Ambitions to remind yourself how you want to stretch yourself. What do you need to act on this quarter given your ambitions? What will success this quarter look like both personally and professionally?

Ambitions	Success
	Personal
	Professional

What's your focus for the quarter? What are your top 3 priorities across your personal and professional life? Also look back to Section 3: My 12-Month Planner and consider what from your calendar is important to note that will require your attention.

Top 3 Priorities	Calendar Notes
Personal	
Professional	

How will you sustain yourself this quarter? Review from Section 2 your Life+Work Resilience Rx. For the left page here, review sections: My Treatment, Take With, and Refill. For the next page, review sections Contraindications and Extra Strength.

QUARTER 4 - Months _____ , _____ , _____	
Value Activities	
Energizing Activities	
Sustaining Activities	
Pauses & Breaks	

*Consider different elements of your Rx: ways to live your values, setting bound-aries, new habits and rituals, sustaining activities, addressing energizers

Given what you're trying to achieve and how you'll stretch yourself this quarter, fill in the sections below to aim your quarter in the right direction to make it sustainable. Remember that we won't always have balance, so consider how you will support yourself to show up at your best.

QUARTER 4 - Months _____ , _____ , _____	
Boundaries	
Structures	
Support	
Try & Practice	

and drainers, productivity hacks or behaviors, making time for fun, or work and home structure to support your life+work resilience.

What's your aim for each month? Based on your Quarter Plan and Quarter Rx, now break down the important actions and activities for each month in the quarter. Make note of anything important on your calendar and what you expect your pace to be to plan accordingly.

	Month 10:
Ambition: Prioritized Actions	
Rx: Prioritized Activities	
Calendar Notes	
Pace	
Other Notes	

Month 11:	Month 12:

What are your actions? Use the Month/Day tracker for awareness building and supporting your commitment to act and build your life+work resilience. Each day, quickly run through and put a check mark by day in the boxes that are relevant for you. Over the month, what do you notice?

Month 10:	1	2	3	4	5	6	7	8	9	10	11	12
My Best Self: I was able to operate at my best today												
Energy: My energy level was good today												
Focus: I was focused on the right activities in alignment with my priorities												
Boundaries: I set boundaries today												
Sustain: I did something to sustain myself												
Pause: I took a pause or break today												
Practice: I practiced what I said I'd test out												
Grace: I gave myself or someone else grace												
Bad At: I allowed myself to be bad at something												
Support: I asked for support or help												

13	14	15	16	17	18	19	20	21	22	23	24	25	26	27	28	29	30	31

Month 11:	1	2	3	4	5	6	7	8	9	10	11	12
My Best Self: I was able to operate at my best today												
Energy: My energy level was good today												
Focus: I was focused on the right activities in alignment with my priorities												
Boundaries: I set boundaries today												
Sustain: I did something to sustain myself												
Pause: I took a pause or break today												
Practice: I practiced what I said I'd test out												
Grace: I gave myself or someone else grace												
Bad At: I allowed myself to be bad at something												
Support: I asked for support or help												

13	14	15	16	17	18	19	20	21	22	23	24	25	26	27	28	29	30	31

Month 12:	1	2	3	4	5	6	7	8	9	10	11	12
My Best Self: I was able to operate at my best today												
Energy: My energy level was good today												
Focus: I was focused on the right activities in alignment with my priorities												
Boundaries: I set boundaries today												
Sustain: I did something to sustain myself												
Pause: I took a pause or break today												
Practice: I practiced what I said I'd test out												
Grace: I gave myself or someone else grace												
Bad At: I allowed myself to be bad at something												
Support: I asked for support or help												

13	14	15	16	17	18	19	20	21	22	23	24	25	26	27	28	29	30	31

How is it going? At the end of each month, fill in the Month Review to track your progress, assessing how you are doing and determining how to adapt along the way.

Month 10: _____

What's working? What's not working?

How would you rate the following dimensions with 1 = low and 5 = high?

Life Satisfaction						Pace				
1 ▢	2 ▢	3 ▢	4 ▢	5 ▢		1 ▢	2 ▢	3 ▢	4 ▢	5 ▢

Life Satisfaction   Pace
1 ▢ 2 ▢ 3 ▢ 4 ▢ 5 ▢   1 ▢ 2 ▢ 3 ▢ 4 ▢ 5 ▢

Work Satisfaction   Resilience
1 ▢ 2 ▢ 3 ▢ 4 ▢ 5 ▢   1 ▢ 2 ▢ 3 ▢ 4 ▢ 5 ▢

Sustainable   Energy
1 ▢ 2 ▢ 3 ▢ 4 ▢ 5 ▢   1 ▢ 2 ▢ 3 ▢ 4 ▢ 5 ▢

Ambition   Productivity
1 ▢ 2 ▢ 3 ▢ 4 ▢ 5 ▢   1 ▢ 2 ▢ 3 ▢ 4 ▢ 5 ▢

Values   Work Structures
1 ▢ 2 ▢ 3 ▢ 4 ▢ 5 ▢   1 ▢ 2 ▢ 3 ▢ 4 ▢ 5 ▢

Priorities   Life Structures
1 ▢ 2 ▢ 3 ▢ 4 ▢ 5 ▢   1 ▢ 2 ▢ 3 ▢ 4 ▢ 5 ▢

What have I learned?

_____

_____

_____

_____

Month 11: _____

What's working? What's not working?

How would you rate the following dimensions with 1 = low and 5 = high?

Life Satisfaction
1 □   2 □   3 □   4 □   5 □

Pace
1 □   2 □   3 □   4 □   5 □

Work Satisfaction
1 □   2 □   3 □   4 □   5 □

Resilience
1 □   2 □   3 □   4 □   5 □

Sustainable
1 □   2 □   3 □   4 □   5 □

Energy
1 □   2 □   3 □   4 □   5 □

Ambition
1 □   2 □   3 □   4 □   5 □

Productivity
1 □   2 □   3 □   4 □   5 □

Values
1 □   2 □   3 □   4 □   5 □

Work Structures
1 □   2 □   3 □   4 □   5 □

Priorities
1 □   2 □   3 □   4 □   5 □

Life Structures
1 □   2 □   3 □   4 □   5 □

What have I learned?

_____

_____

_____

_____

_____

_____

_____

Month 12: _____

What's working? What's not working?

How would you rate the following dimensions with 1 = low and 5 = high?

Life Satisfaction
1 □   2 □   3 □   4 □   5 □

Pace
1 □   2 □   3 □   4 □   5 □

Work Satisfaction
1 □   2 □   3 □   4 □   5 □

Resilience
1 □   2 □   3 □   4 □   5 □

Sustainable
1 □   2 □   3 □   4 □   5 □

Energy
1 □   2 □   3 □   4 □   5 □

Ambition
1 □   2 □   3 □   4 □   5 □

Productivity
1 □   2 □   3 □   4 □   5 □

Values
1 □   2 □   3 □   4 □   5 □

Work Structures
1 □   2 □   3 □   4 □   5 □

Priorities
1 □   2 □   3 □   4 □   5 □

Life Structures
1 □   2 □   3 □   4 □   5 □

What have I learned?

_____

_____

_____

_____

_____

_____

_____

How did it go? At the end of the quarter, fill in the Quarter Review to assess how the quarter went and to identify opportunities to adapt next quarter.

Quarter 4: _____

What's working? What's not working?

How would you rate the following dimensions with 1 = low and 5 = high?

Life Satisfaction
1 □   2 □   3 □   4 □   5 □

Pace
1 □   2 □   3 □   4 □   5 □

Work Satisfaction
1 □   2 □   3 □   4 □   5 □

Resilience
1 □   2 □   3 □   4 □   5 □

Sustainable
1 □   2 □   3 □   4 □   5 □

Energy
1 □   2 □   3 □   4 □   5 □

Ambition
1 □   2 □   3 □   4 □   5 □

Productivity
1 □   2 □   3 □   4 □   5 □

Values
1 □   2 □   3 □   4 □   5 □

Work Structures
1 □   2 □   3 □   4 □   5 □

Priorities
1 □   2 □   3 □   4 □   5 □

Life Structures
1 □   2 □   3 □   4 □   5 □

What have I learned?

_____

_____

_____

_____

What worked?

_____

_____

_____

_____

What didn't work?

_____

_____

_____

_____

What was unsustainable?

_____

_____

_____

_____

What do you want to do differently next quarter?

_____

_____

_____

_____

What I've learned about myself...

_____

_____

_____

New boundaries I want to set are...

_____

_____

_____

New work structures I want to set are...

_____

_____

_____

New home structures I want to set are...

_____

_____

_____

What I also want to try and practice next are...

_____

_____

_____

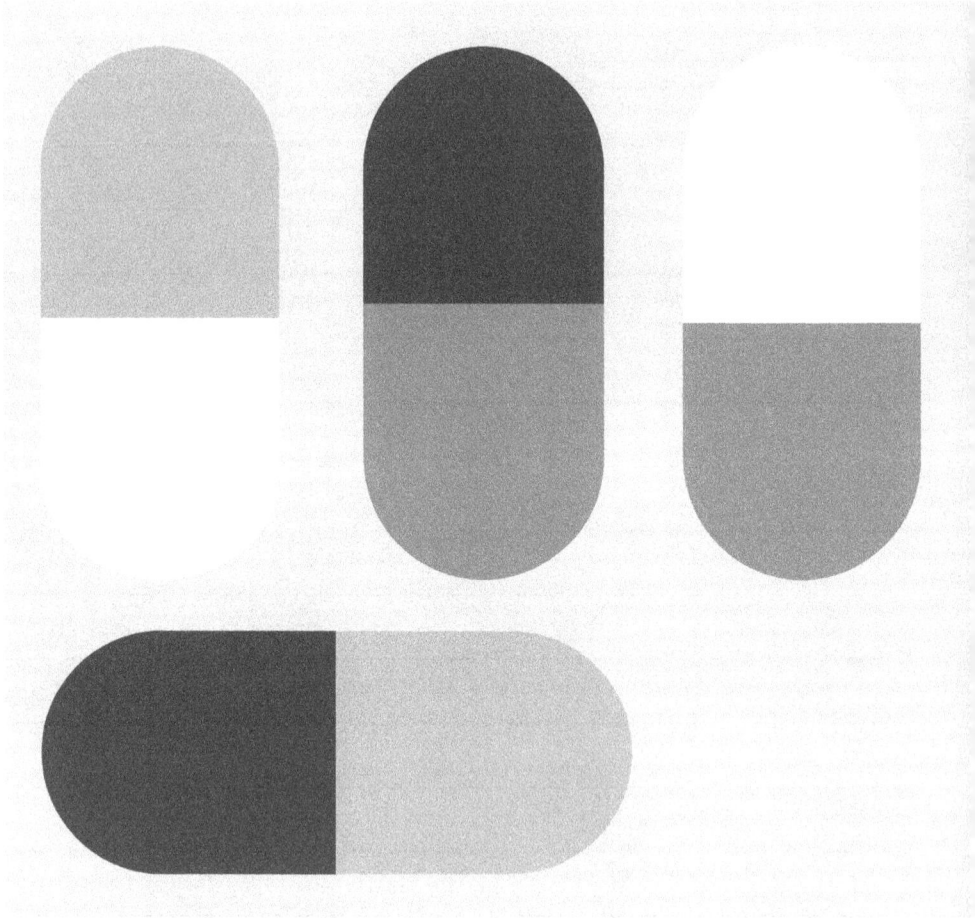

I'll stay committed to...

_____

_____

_____

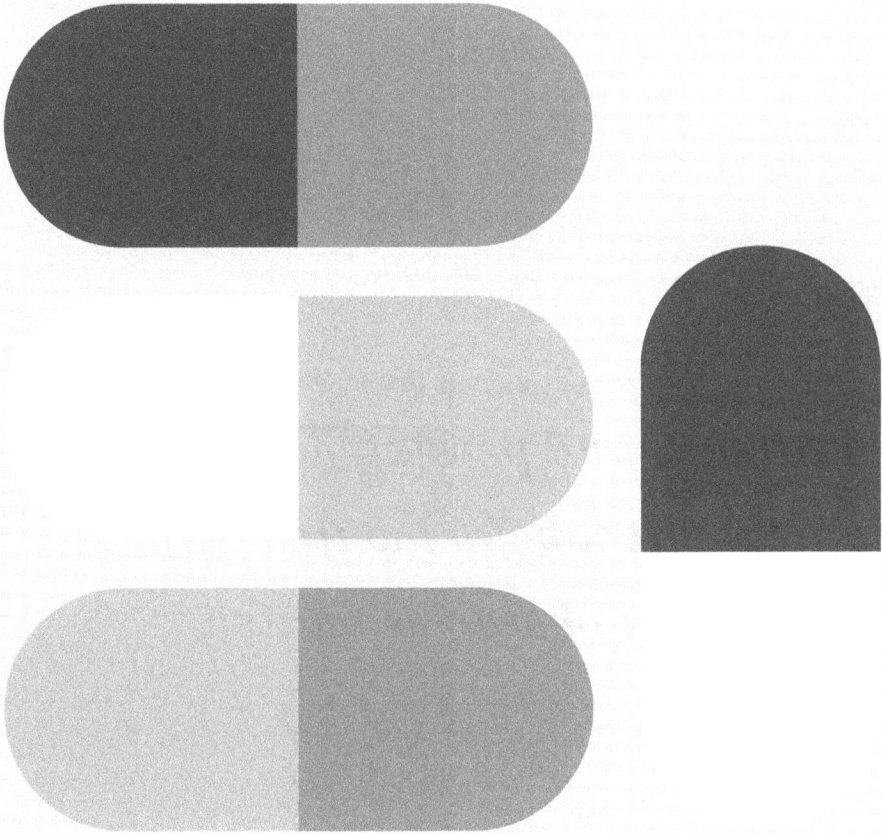

Weekly & Daily

Check-Ins

"Patience and persistence have a magical effect before which difficulties and obstacles vanish."

JOHN QUINCY ADAMS

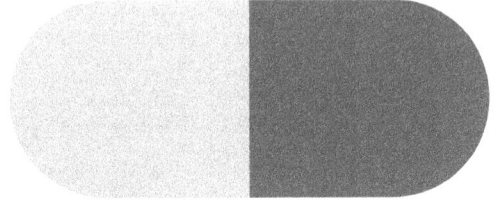

Need reminders to help you stay on-track in building your sustainable and ambitious life+work? Each week and day, review your Ambitions and Life+Work Resilience Rx responses and use these 5-questions as reminders to stay in alignment with your intentions and to build your life+work resilience.

Remember, it's a practice that calls for perspective, personalization, pacing, and patience. And that means it isn't easy! It takes learning about ourselves, planning, practicing, and progressing.

And, you got this!

Weekly Sustainable Ambition Check-In

What are my top priorities for the week? Am I working on the right things that will forward my goals and align with my values?

What can I cut from my to-do list? What can I simplify?

What can I do to help me operate at my best this week?

What do I need to put on the calendar first?

When do I have times for pauses, breaks, and sustaining activities?

Daily Sustainable Ambition Check-In

○ What is my energy level today and what kind of effort can I put into my work and life?

○ What do I need to support myself to show up as my best self today?

○ What are the ways I will take a pause today of any length—in 30 seconds, 2 minutes, 15-30 minutes, 1 hour+?

○ What is the 1 thing I must get done today professionally? personally?

○ What are at least 3 projects or tasks I can cut from my list professionally? personally?

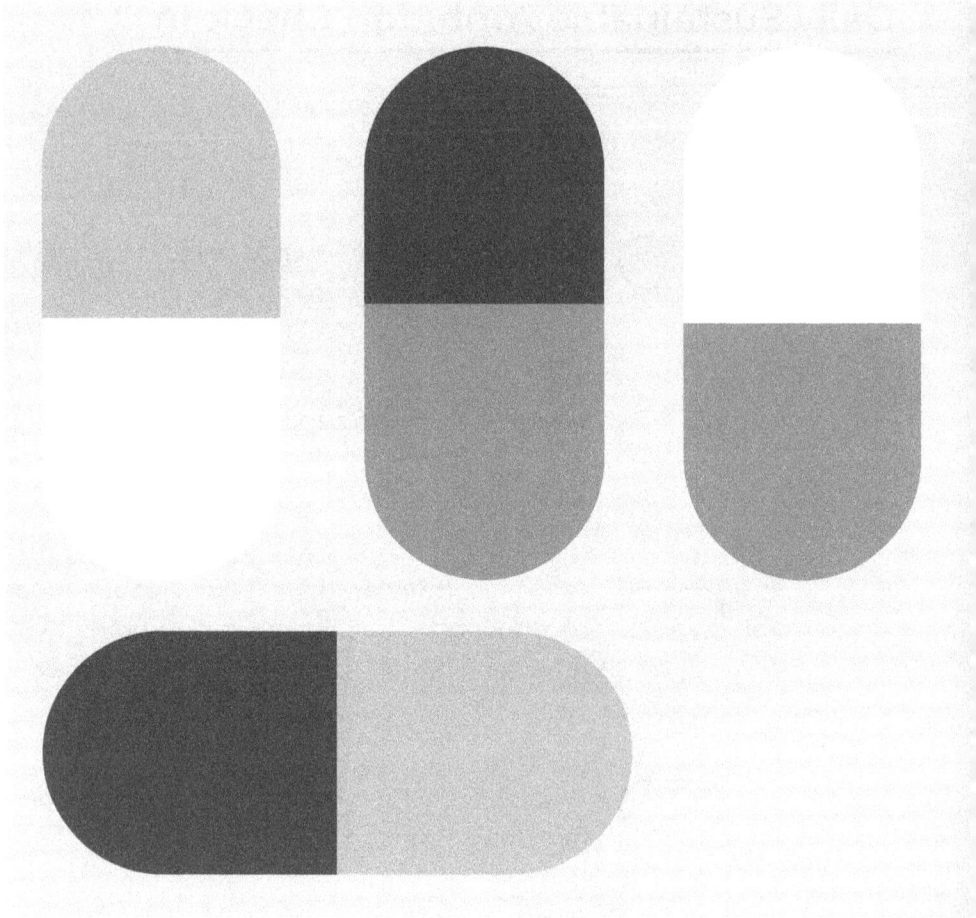

The last 12 months were...

_____

_____

_____

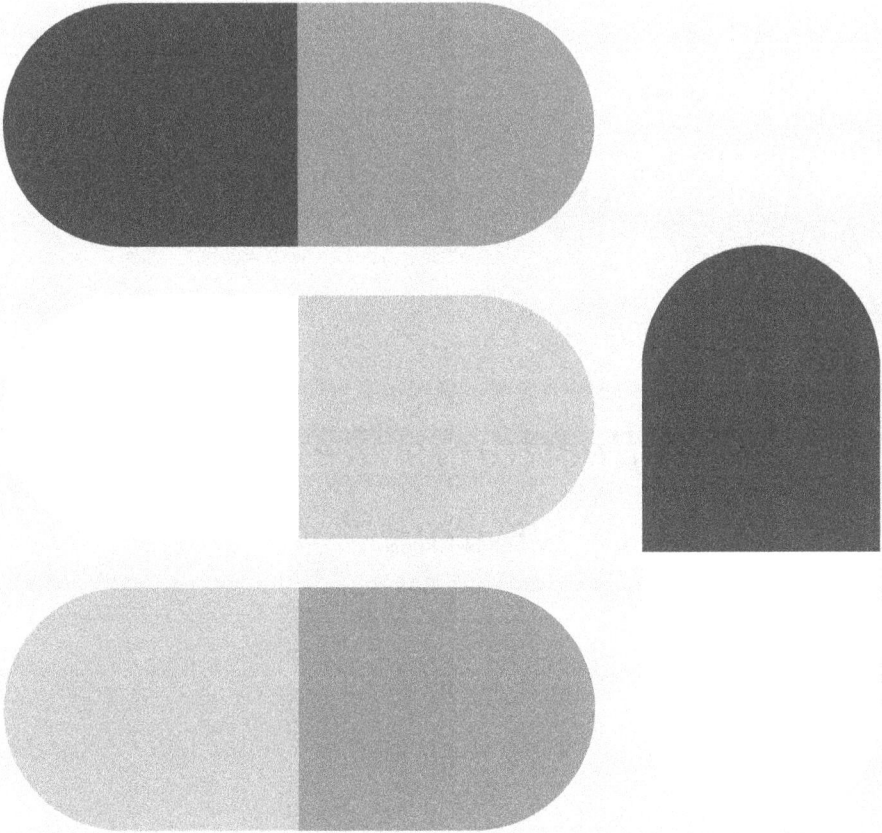

12-Month Review

"Self-reflection is the school of wisdom."

BALTASAR GRACIAN

You made it! And we hope this workbook+planner helped make it a more sustainable 12 months for you.

As you close this time, find some space to reflect. It's an important step in the process to both honor the time you just lived and unlock your personal wisdom to give you insight to inform the coming 6 and 12 months ahead.

As with the Month and Quarter Reviews, when you reflect on the full 12 months, what did you learn? What worked, what didn't, what's next?

While having sustainability in one's life+work is a constant practice, continue to aspire! Own your time and be in choice to build a more sustainable life+work. Since our lives and the world around us aren't static, take this learning to help you optimize your Life+Work Resilience Rx to support you in the months ahead.

Let's see what wisdom and learning is here for you.

Take a little time to reflect. What can you learn from the past 12 months that can set you up for a more sustainable 12 months ahead? What were the major milestones and events across your personal and professional life? When you look back to Section 1: My Ambitions, how did you do against your Ambitions, Purpose, and Priorities? What wins

Month/Year _____ to Month/Year _____

Mos 1-3	Mos 4-6

Overall Observations

do you want to acknowledge and celebrate? When you look back to Section 2 and your Life+Work Resilience Rx and Section 3: My 12 Month Planner, what is worthy to note? What do you notice and what can you acknowledge around building a more sustainable life+work in the last 12 months?

Mos 7-9	Mos 10-12

How did it go? Fill in the 12-Month Review to assess how the 12 months went and to identify opportunities to adapt in the coming months.

What's worked? What didn't work?

How would you rate the following dimensions with 1 = low and 5 = high?

Life Satisfaction

1 □   2 □   3 □   4 □   5 □

Pace

1 □   2 □   3 □   4 □   5 □

Work Satisfaction

1 □   2 □   3 □   4 □   5 □

Resilience

1 □   2 □   3 □   4 □   5 □

Sustainable

1 □   2 □   3 □   4 □   5 □

Energy

1 □   2 □   3 □   4 □   5 □

Ambition

1 □   2 □   3 □   4 □   5 □

Productivity

1 □   2 □   3 □   4 □   5 □

Values

1 □   2 □   3 □   4 □   5 □

Work Structures

1 □   2 □   3 □   4 □   5 □

Priorities

1 □   2 □   3 □   4 □   5 □

Life Structures

1 □   2 □   3 □   4 □   5 □

What worked?

_____

_____

_____

_____

_____

_____

What didn't work?

_____

_____

_____

_____

_____

_____

What was unsustainable?

_____

_____

_____

_____

_____

_____

What I've learned about myself...

_____

_____

_____

What I want to take into the next 12 months...

_____

_____

_____

What I want to do differently in the next 12 months...

_____

_____

_____

Work structures I want to keep are...

_____

_____

_____

Home structures I want to keep are...

_____

_____

_____

I am ready to...

_____

_____

_____

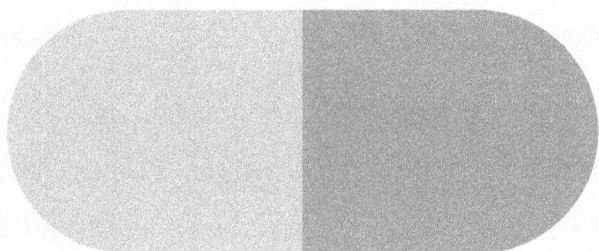

What's Next?

"Life can only be understood backward, but it must be lived forwards."

SØREN KIERKEGAARD

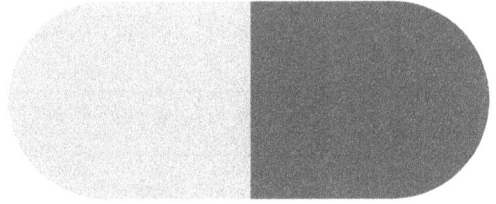

As we said at the beginning of the workbook+planner, Sustainable Ambition is aspirational. It asks us to hold two opposing ideas—sustain and stretch—at the same time. How can we sustain ourselves (sustainable), while stretching ourselves (ambition)? That implies it is a practice that calls for perspective, personalization, pacing, and patience. And that means it isn't easy! It takes learning about ourselves, planning, practicing, and progressing.

With the discipline you've demonstrated this year, you've learned about yourself and practiced your Life+Work Resilience Rx to help you show up as your best self and to create a life+work that is more sustainable over time.

With the learning you've had these past twelve months, what's next as you look to both sustain and stretch yourself in the next six, twelve, and eighteen months ahead? Set your ambition and intentions, rewrite your Life+Work Resilience Rx, and get into action.

We encourage you to keep learning about yourself and keep planning, practicing, and progressing. You can take back control and be in choice to build a more sustainable life+work.

_____

_____

_____

_____

_____

_____

_____

_____

_____

_____

_____

_____

_____

_____

_____

_____

_____

_____

_____

_____

_____

_____

_____

_____

_____

_____

_____

_____

_____

_____

_____

_____

_____

_____

_____

_____

_____

For resources that complement the workbook+planner go to:

www.sustainableambition.com/planner

We love feedback!

We want to make sure we create value for you. If you have feedback on how to make the workbook+planner even better, please let us know! Contact us at info@sustainableambition.com. We'd be very grateful!

Want to stay connected to Sustainable Ambition?

Learn more at: SustainableAmbition.com

Sign-up for the newsletter at: SustainableAmbition.com/subscribe

Listen to The Sustainable Ambition Podcast on your favorite podcast player.

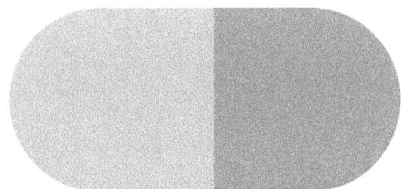

About the Author

Kathy Oneto is a strategy executive and life+work and executive coach who bridges her two worlds bringing strategic thinking to life+work planning and management. She is the founder of Sustainable Ambition and host of The Sustainable Ambition Podcast. Her mission is to help people attain more joy, satisfaction, and fulfillment in their careers from decade to decade, helping them to be ambitious with more ease and without burnout. She holds an MBA from Berkeley's Haas School of Business and a BS in Commerce from the University of Virginia. Kathy lives in San Francisco with her husband and the fog.

CPSIA information can be obtained
at www.ICGtesting.com
Printed in the USA
LVHW010353110122
708210LV00005B/260